"Loray Daws's *Introduction t* a wide aperture into the spiri .... his many colors and voices: poet, psychotherapist, *Tzadik*, orphic visionary, and breather of psychic life. More than simply an introduction, Daws's work on Eigen's oeuvre is both a profound academic resource and an extension of the wisdom tradition they both share. One finds emotional and spiritual truths quoted from a vast array of Eigen's work as part of an arc and trajectory that expresses deep love for how we touch each other's insides."

Robin Bagai, Psy.D., *Author of "Michael Eigen and Evolution of Psyche"*

"Loray Daws has a developing international reputation as a scholar-practitioner whose interests cover the full range of psychoanalytic praxis and theory. In this volume, which without hyperbole can be describes as brilliant, Daws provides the first introductory text to one of the most significant figures in contemporary psychoanalysis. He is the right person to have done this and there is no doubt that he is up to the task. The core concerns of Eigen are articulated with singular clarity. At the same time the experienced Eigen reader is opened to dimensions and nuances which they may not have previously realized. While clearly basing Eigen's work in a Elkin-Winnicott-Bion field, Daws also locates it a broader psychoanalytic context (for example Bollas, Balint) thereby helping the reader sense where Eigen fits in. The writing is both emotionally in touch and intellectually rigorous. This is a palpably alive book which reveals the sheer fecundity of Eigen's work."

Stephen Bloch, *Jungian Psychoanalyst, Editor of "Living Moments: On the Work of Michael Eigen" and "Music and Psyche"*

"Over the past forty years, Michael Eigen's voluminous and evocative writing – intriguing, profoundly moving, and challenging – connects us with the fundamental psychic realities of psychoanalytic treatment and human sensibilities, pain, suffering and faith. It is a living process emerging from the very act of experiencing, feeling, and sharing. Loray Daws' *Introduction to Michael Eigen* offers us a thoughtful, telling, and engaging exploration of the most essential themes of Eigen's writing. The reader is in for a thorough and enriching journey into Eigen's unique psychoanalytic world."

Ofra Eshel, *faculty, training and supervising analyst of the Israel Psychoanalytic Society, honorary member of the New Center for Psychoanalysis, Los Angeles*

Michael Eigen

This insightful book critically reviews and presents an accessible introduction to the life and work of one of the most celebrated modern psychoanalysts, Michael Eigen.

With work spanning over five decades, countless articles, and 30 published book volumes, Daws explores Eigen's main works through key themes and concepts, such as working with our psychotic core, psychic deadness, primary affects, and the need for spirituality for practicing psychoanalysts. The book covers Eigen's early life and formative clinical years, explores his rereading of Freud, Jung and Lacan, and lastly covers Eigen's Seoul seminars, the impact of trauma, the importance of faith and the use of Kabbalah as a framework for analysis.

This book will not only engage the first-time Eigen reader, but will also be of much interest to the experienced psychologist and psychoanalyst already familiar with Eigen's work.

Loray Daws is a registered Clinical Psychologist in South Africa and British Columbia, Canada. He is currently in private practice and serves as Senior Faculty Member at the International Masterson Institute in New York, and specializes in psychoanalysis and daseinsanalysis. He is the editor of four books in psychoanalysis and existential analysis.

Routledge Introductions to Contemporary Psychoanalysis

Aner Govrin, Ph.D.
Series Editor

Tair Caspi, Ph.D.
Executive Editor

Yael Peri Herzovich
Assistant Editor

"Routledge Introductions to Contemporary Psychoanalysis" is one of the prominent psychoanalytic publishing ventures of our day. It will comprise dozens of books that will serve as concise introductions dedicated to influential concepts, theories, leading figures, and techniques in psychoanalysis covering every important aspect of psychoanalysis.

The length of each book is fixed at 40,000 words.

The series' books are designed to be easily accessible to provide informative answers in various areas of psychoanalytic thought. Each book will provide updated ideas on topics relevant to contemporary psychoanalysis – from the unconscious and dreams, projective identification and eating disorders, through neuropsychoanalysis, colonialism, and spiritual-sensitive psychoanalysis. Books will also be dedicated to prominent figures in the field, such as Melanie Klein, Jaque Lacan, Sandor Ferenczi, Otto Kernberg, and Michael Eigen.

Not serving solely as an introduction for beginners, the purpose of the series is to offer compendiums of information on particular topics within different psychoanalytic schools. We ask authors to review a topic but also address the readers with their own personal views and contribution to the specific chosen field. Books will make intricate ideas comprehensible without compromising their complexity.

We aim to make contemporary psychoanalysis more accessible to both clinicians and the general educated public.

Transgender Identities: A Contemporary Introduction
Alessandra Lemma

Projective Identification: A Contemporary Introduction
Robert Waska

Donald Meltzer: A Contemporary Introduction
Meg Harris Williams

Michael Eigen

A Contemporary Introduction

Loray Daws

Routledge
Taylor & Francis Group

LONDON AND NEW YORK

Cover image: © Michal Heiman, *Asylum 1855–2020, The Sleeper* (video, psychoanalytic sofa and Plate 34), exhibition view, Herzliya Museum of Contemporary Art, 2017

First published 2023
by Routledge
4 Park Square, Milton Park, Abingdon, Oxon OX14 4RN

and by Routledge
605 Third Avenue, New York, NY 10158

Routledge is an imprint of the Taylor & Francis Group, an informa business

British Library Cataloguing-in-Publication Data
A catalogue record for this book is available from the British Library

Library of Congress Cataloging-in-Publication Data
Names: Daws, Loray, author.
Title: Michael Eigen : A Contemporary Introduction / Loray Daws.
Description: New York, NY : Routledge, 2023. |
Series: Routledge introductions to contemporary psychoanalysis |
Includes bibliographical references and index.
Identifiers: LCCN 2022009640 | ISBN 9780367433901 (paperback) |
ISBN 9780367433895 (hardback) | ISBN 9781003002871 (ebook)
Subjects: LCSH: Eigen, Michael. | Psychoanalysis.
Classification: LCC BF109.E54 D39 2023 |
DDC 150.19/5–dc23/eng/20220509
LC record available at https://lccn.loc.gov/2022009640

ISBN: 9780367433895 (hbk)
ISBN: 9780367433901 (pbk)
ISBN: 9781003002871 (ebk)

DOI: 10.4324/9781003002871

Typeset in Times New Roman
by Newgen Publishing UK

For Father

Lechol Nefesh

Tehom el Tehom Korei...
Deep call unto Deep....
Psalm 42:8

Contents

Foreword by Dr. Michael Eigen

I am deeply moved that Loray Daws has read my work so thoroughly and translated it into an introduction that may touch many individuals and possibly help bring them closer to themselves. It is an intimate work involved in what James Hillman (1997) might call soul creation (his term was "soul-making"). Daws touches and opens daily adventures of psychic transformations that often play a subterranean role in psychic growth over a lifetime. I should say psychic growth and its vicissitudes because deformations and setbacks can play a vital part in renewal.

My own work has long emphasized complexities of self-other and mind-body relations. Daws not only brings out relational nuances in my work but adds to them. It is as if he uses my work like an artist might use his palette to open further dimensions of experience, life colors calling for use and care. The reader can expect to dip into my work then suddenly find him or herself in unanticipated depths joining psychic hungers, longings, and hopes. The reading itself will be an opening of wells within, a stimulus for the reader's contact with the depths. There will be much opportunity for didactic learning, but my sense is there is also a deeper value for fertile meetings of author, reader, and the work itself engaged in spontaneous interweaving.

I've often written about the evolutionary task of becoming partners with our capacities rather than merely succumbing to a control-mastery model. We need both our curiosity and exploratory drives as well as an ability to be still and experience ourselves at rest in quietude. The Biblical God appears with thunder and lightning but also a still, small voice, inaudible and invisible yet ineffably moving, opening soul dimensions. All our capacities potentially have something to give us and through us others. I hope you will find in this work a vehicle for this receiving – giving that you will further in your own way, a replenishing that can go on all lifelong.

Reference

Hillman, J. (1997). *Re-Visualizing Psychology*. New York: William Morrow.

About the author

Loray Daws is a registered Clinical Psychologist in both South Africa and British Columbia, Canada. He is currently in private practice and serves as a Senior Faculty member at the International Masterson Institute in New York. He has published and works in the areas of psychoanalysis, daseinsanalysis, psychoanalytic psychotherapy, disorders of the self, psychosomatic difficulties, mental health ethics, and the Rorschach. He also serves as assistant editor for the *Global Journal of Health Sciences* in Canada, evaluator and international advisory board member for the *International Journal of Psychotherapy*, assistant editor for *EPIS* (*Existential Psychoanalytic Institute and Society*), and both teaches and supervises in South Africa, Australia, and Turkey in the psychoanalytic approach to disorders of the self. He is the editor of four books on psychoanalysis and existential analysis.

Preface

To be asked to write an introductory text on the work of Dr. Michael Eigen remains a singular privilege and soul gift. Optimism was soon flooded with anxiety as Eigen's work represents a phenomenologically rich and distinct psychoanalytic vision. Psychoanalysts such as James Grotstein, Adam Phillips, Ofra Eshel, and many others have referred to Eigen as a modern-day psychoanalytic mystic,[1] a mythopoetic voice able to create a body of psychoanalytic work infused with rare moral and emotional seriousness. Returning to Eigen's countless texts over many years has never ceased to fill me with wonder, allowing me as a reader to sample, taste, and feel out various psychological realities, all without any demand to master a singular structure[2] of thought. Eigen himself states:

> From the outset, it seemed clear that I would never be a strictly orthodox analyst, whatever that may mean.
>
> (1993, p. 261)

> A good many voices compete in my inner space ... Differentiated gestalts evolve through a long immersion in an area of interest.
>
> (1986, p. 27)

> No attempt is made to be exhaustive or definitive...
>
> (1986, pp. 87–88)

> The impact of the patient is translated into guesses or convictions about what is happening. The situation is both Kantian and mystical.
>
> (1986, p. 136)

Given such a rich tapestry of creativity and thought spanning over five decades, countless articles, and more than 30 books, I decided to limit the current introductory explorations to a few chosen central themes as found in five thematic epochs. I have to confess I do not read Eigen like I do James F. Masterson. Eigen's work cannot be manualized, codified, or structured in a strict academic sense. As part of *wisdom literature*, any structuralization would be mortifying to Eigen's rich thinking, ossifying his psychoanalytic work that relies on cultivating our own psychic taste buds.[3] As such, over the many years, I have naturally "read" and "approached" Eigen's writing and thought similar to reading poetry or spiritual texts. I turn and return to Eigen's words, concepts, sentences, thoughts, feelings and "build" round them, furnishing Eigen's nodal thinking with my own psychoanalytic growth (which is unending). Given the task set by editors and the sections to follow, it will be inevitable that "Eigen" here is written *more academically* for this preliminary work. For that, I apologize to Dr. Eigen. As defined in spiritual traditions, I hope my attempt at a more *circumambulating approach* seems most evident as I read this as inherent to Eigen's world-self-other touch. Hopefully, what may shine through is a psychoanalysis more akin in process to the soul-felt dedication by Marie Cardinal in her book *The Words to say it* (1983) in which she wrote as dedication: *"To the doctor who helped me be born."*

Notes

1 See as example Eigen's *Ecstacy*: "The age of incessant recombinations has begun, the age that creates new elements. Everything mates with everything else. Get used to strange births." (2001, p. 12).

2 *Dan*: What I like is you don't try to pin me. You don't say this is you and that's that. You don't say that's the real thing and that isn't..." (2002, p. 104).

3 For a felt sense review Eigen in *Seoul, Volume 1: Madness and Murder,* question 5 on day 2 (2010, p. 53).

Acknowledgments

I am deeply indebted to Drs. Aner Govrin and Tair Caspi for approaching me to write an introductory text on Michael Eigen's work. It has been a singular pleasure, and I am grateful for their sensitive, immensely supportive, and wise editorial support.

To Ilan Amir and Gaby Shefler (2020) for introducing me, indirectly through a podcast, to the "Lechol Nefesh" Project.

Routledge for the opportunity to write an introductory work on Michael Eigen as well as their creative vision in both housing and furthering Michael Eigen's work. Deep gratitude to Ms Katie Randall, editorial assistant, for invaluable feedback and navigating the publication process, as well as Ms Annette Day, permissions administrator, T&F Book Permissions, Taylor & Francis Group, for their gracious permission to use Eigen's work as epigraphs.

Ms Suzanna Tamminen, Director and Editor in Chief, Wesleyan University Press for their permission to use Eigen's work as epigraphs.

Ms Penny Kokot-Louw for a flawless translation of Andre P. Brink's work as it appeared in 1967.

Dr. Michael Eigen for his unending support and willingness to write the foreword to the book.

Ms Keri Cohen for reading the manuscript and many heartfelt and helpful suggestions. I remain indebted.

To my own background of support: my family, many colleagues, too many to mention, and my analysts over 20 years (Drs Assie Gildenhuys, A. C. N. Preller, and Janet Oakes). Autochthonous creation, inner freedom, and stepping forth is only possible through others. I remain deeply indebted and appreciative to all.

To the various analysands who graciously provided me with material for this volume. Your work serves us all.

Part I

Being-with Eigen

Psychotherapy plays a vital role in ensuring that those who struggle in the night do not do so in vain.

(Eigen, 1999, p. x)

As in all my work, my desire is not to "solve" anything, but to open fields of experiencing. Perhaps my desire is to touch the thing itself, to let it touch us with all it can do.

(Eigen, 2007, p. 130)

DOI: 10.4324/9781003002871-1

Chapter 1

Introduction to healing longing and the ever-healing wound

My portraits are concerned with letting feeling storms speak, letting them have their say, seeing where they lead. The kind of "read" I hope for, the kind of writing I do, is a kind of "training" or invitation to stay with experience without pressing the eject button too quickly... At this point in our history it is critical to develop an ability to taste storm nuances before they flame and learn how to communicate within the storm's heart.

(Eigen, 2005, pp. 9–10)

Introduction

Eigen's voluminous psychoanalytic writing forges a unique, if not orphic, approach to our perennial soul disquiet.[1] As such, encompassing all of Eigen's prolific thinking into a single volume would be an impossible task. Profound, poetic, and singularly transformative, Eigen's writing spans more than 30 psychoanalytic volumes and countless articles articulating the importance of each individual's *psychological birth and rebirth capacity, feeling psychologically alive despite embryonic psychic equipment, surviving toxic and nourishing evolution within our distinction–union structure, making psychological use of our aliveness–deadness dialectic, and the therapeutic difficulties encountered within, and by, the analytic pair given the destructive and creative force(s) within.* Eigen's psychoanalytic prose, reveries, and technical approach remain written expressions of felt soul language, a language seemingly closer to prayer – a voice and thinking found in mystical traditions, intrinsically evocative.

I have told the story ... of many people who opened themselves to what they most feared and those who were unable to. There is music, color, and mystery in both the opening and closing...

(Eigen, 1999, p. x)

DOI: 10.4324/9781003002871-2

To not cultivate the feel of another is a kind of soul murder. The evolution of the human race depends on not aborting the feeling of another.

(2005, p. 21)

More is involved than the capacity to know... A capacity as deep or deeper than the sense of catastrophe must be called forth if healing or profound change is to occur.

(1993, p. 219)

This kind of therapy involves commitment to deep experiencing... *There is support deeper than anything one can hold onto.*

(2004, pp. 170–171)

With every volume published, Eigen moves incisively and imperceptibly closer to the transformative language of the inviolable I, the sensitive self, our felt emotional storms, and *the importance of faith* in psychological transformations. By *awakening* our embryonic capacities to the multitude of undercurrents as experienced by the *autochthonous and inviolable I,* it is believed that psychic impacts may be transformed in ways that enhance self-experience and a sense of coherence.[2] Thus, remaining committed to Eigen's texts, one may come to find oneself moved ever so subtly, imperceptibly, if not infinitesimally closer to the creative currents that inform one's idiom and *being* ontologically. Eigen's psychoanalysis can undoubtedly be viewed an ontological psychoanalysis.

In the beginning: *transformative* aspects of pathological tendencies, being unwanted, and our psychotic core

Eigen's psychoanalytic sojourns into the *inviolable I* gives special attention to the difficulties *coming-into-being-with* entails as the "I" experiences numerous mind–body–other splits throughout its development. Working with severely detached and unwanted patients, as well as entrenched states of mind, Eigen's psychoanalytic vision[3] provides unique insights into (a) the positive aspects of pathological tendencies, (b) the importance of psychological indwelling as kenosis ("letting go," "self-emptying"), (c) transformational self-experiences to remain known and unknown (a Winnicott–Eigen dialectic), (d) the developmental need for ideal images, (e) the significance of cultivating a catastrophe–faith dialectic, (f) the importance of working with demonized aspects of self, and (g) responding to, and within, self–other states of omnipotence, mindlessness–selflessness, and omniscience. These starting points served as a creative foundation to my reading of Eigen's foundational ethnopoieinic (i.e., the formation or transformation of one's own mode of existence) *first psychoanalytic epoch*; in a mere 16 years of writing, Eigen's poiesis finds a unique, integrative approach to our injured *primordial sense of self as "more than" exclusively pathological and passive*, despite overt expressions in problems of living, that is, as found in psychotic processes, schizoid adaptations, psychopathy (psyche-hardening), and excessive self-drivenness. Deracinated subjectivities and the purloined *self* find a singular psychoanalytic voice able to remain steadfastly faithful to the psyche's primordial capacity for *psychological gestation and "re"-birth*[4] despite the damage. Textually speaking, Eigen's psychoanalytic imagination serves as a hopeful and devoted guardian, if not a servant, to the process of transformation (rebirth) in a *Rhythm of Faith* (Eigen, 2005). Reading Eigen's initial conceptualizations (1973–1986) immediately evoked for me various descriptions of sensitive analysands articulating psyche-damage, fateful adaptations, recovery rhythms and needs, and much more.

> *Analysand*: This therapy process ... it is like when you have a damaged plant, a cutting. You need a small container with water. You cannot just stick the cutting or damaged root into the ground. Not even if the soil is fertile. So in one, you have rooting hormone. Touch the tip of a cutting in the hormone, and then place in the other container with water. Don't give the cutting too much hormone; once it touches, it is activated. Now it needs time, the holding of the water.

> *Analysand*: This process is akin to much-needed dialysis, my psychological-psyche dialysis.

> *Analysand*: Therapy is my tamoxifen, blocking my overbearing mother. She was like the "Other Mother" of the story *Caroline*. A cancerous too-muchness.

As with Eigen's writing, the analysands provide rich imagery concerning damage and rebirth possibilities, fertility, and growth despite the damage. The reference to a much-needed psychological-psyche dialysis, or the searching for, and use of another able to detoxify, if not purify, recalls Eigen's ideal images and primary process thinking (*Psychic Deadness*, 1996). Furthermore, the psyche's inherent need for suspension, time, and "not too much" as the rooting hormone activates growth potential is artfully evident in all of Eigen's thinking.[5] A gentle *rooting touch* can undoubtedly go far in activating the inherent growth capacity in the psyche, as with a damaged cutting. Eigen's *containing-rooting-imaginal psyche* focuses on the facticity that our individual and collective nourishment ∞[6] trauma *dialectic* remains perennially in need of psychic development able to sustain painful thinking–feeling transformations if not catastrophic evolutionary impacts without further collapse $\rightleftarrows$ evacuation spirals. Furthermore, at the foundation of all psychological development, if not life in general, and as will be discussed throughout the chapters to follow, we find a *primordial Self* and *primordial Other* entwined within a *distinction–union* experience that remains part of our psychic fabric throughout life, informing our growth–damage spirals. Eigen's books and articles pre-1996 (*Psychic Deadness*) serve as initial *archetypal blueprints* to our shared *primordial-union-distinction-nourishment-trauma impact*(s). Eigen describes our *distinction–union* tendencies as follows:

> In sum, distinction–union tendencies enter into many kinds of relationships with each other, antagonistic, symbiotic, parasitic, nullifying, disconnecting, nourishing. We can always ask what one or other of these tendencies is doing at any moment, as both are always co-present. They implicitly characterize mind-body as well as self-other relations and can be read on many planes, adaptive, psychic, behavioral, individual, sociological, mystic. To be permeable and distinct, connected and separate, in union yet distinct, is part of our plasticity and persistence, part of the mystery, difficulty, and creative challenge of our nature ... *Each strand of our being has a biography. Distinction has its history, so does union, as does their conjunction, their common fate.*
>
> (2011, pp. 15–16; emphasis added)

To articulate our distinction–union biographies, Eigen graciously includes countless psychoanalytic dialogues with analysands as *felt reality* touching the *distinction–union registers*[7] of parental hopes, limitations, failures, and successes. No family is alike, and yet likeness is evident. Duality in union and distinction are constant developmental vertexes. For Eigen, parental care, in essence, primarily reflects a mixture of nourishment–trauma potentiality; optimal and not so optimal love and frustration that serve as psychic bloodstream throughout, as Henry Elkin would write (see Chapter 3), to our *T-ego (mental self)* and *body–ego (body self)* integration.

> Thus love is mixed with a variety of tendencies, including anxious control, worry, death dread, ambition, self-hate. Parental love is not pure ... The child must digest messianic expectations fused with everyday life. To an extent, we learn to use what psychic nutriments we can and avoid what is toxic ... In different measures, no one escapes toxic elements in nourishment secured.
>
> (1999, p. xv)

As such,

> Our real sense of possible disaster is complicated by the fact that psychic life is shaky. *We can fall apart and come together in many different ways*

throughout the day. Some aspects of *body* or *mental self* may be more shaky (or rigid) than others. Rigidity partly compensates for shakiness. We may use some aspects of experience to organize others and hold on to these handles for dear life. *The very birth and growth of personality may be experienced as catastrophic. If we grow enough of a psyche so that we can work decently with ourselves, we may be able to become more or less creative catastrophes.* We need to admit the unevenness of personality development. We remain embryonic throughout our lives.

(1992, p. xvii; emphasis added)

To be touched upon throughout the introductory chapters to come, Eigen's own historical-emotional and psychoanalytic background serves as an example of our unevenness, our psyche as a more or less *creative catastrophe*. Fused within trauma–nourishment tendencies and inventive mixtures, the reader will come to meet the two trees in Eigen's own psychic garden. Eigen's primordial parental unit served as creative soil to a singular sensitivity and psychological capacity in describing our too much–too little dialectic. That is, the too-much–too-little dialectic remains evident throughout Eigen's own development as well as Eigen's faithful psychoanalytic companioning of various psychoanalytic cases. Eigen partners theory and his fellow analytic sojourners with the same "nerve" and sensitivity in locating and describing enlivening and deadening spots as they are scattered throughout the personality. Holding, reimagining, and growing with the Other, Eigen actively engages with, touches upon, and imagines a *unique rhythm of faith* as background support. The result, a transformative imaginal language of our trauma–nourishment bonds and the possibility of a psychic canvas able to sustain transformations in Bion's O. Eigen's *Rhythm of Faith*, in essence, stands in creative relationship with his *Primary Developmental Statements*:

1. *In the beginning* there is nourishment.
2. In the beginning (almost) there is trauma.
3. In the beginning there is nourishment trauma.

(Eigen 1999, p. 145)

As such,

Wounds of childhood are wells on fire. We cap them as we can and harden around them. Sometimes we develop colorful exoskeletons... The link between suffering and aliveness is an intrinsic part of the growth process. If one speaks of birth trauma, one might also speak of fertilization trauma or embryonic growth trauma ... the womb is perfect only in phantasy. Perhaps thumb-sucking in the womb is a reflex to regulate stress, an active attempt as self-soothing, a spontaneous discovery of how to produce pleasure, an attempt to close the circuit and feel whole.

(1995, pp. 190–191)

Coming through and experiencing *renewal* within lack, if not breakdown (trauma) recovery rhythms (being able to lime psychic birth and rebirth potentiality within a rhythm of faith), all partner Eigen's primary statements and are alchemically present in his various theoretical-clinical (1986, 1996, 1999, 2001a, 2001b, 2004, 2016) and case-study volumes (1992, 1995). Paired with Eigen's psychoanalytic companioning is also the rare privilege to read Eigen's open expression of his own development and unfolding as a psychoanalyst. Eigen graciously includes the psychoanalysts and colleagues who have played a pivotal role in his psychoanalytic formation. Given their importance to Eigen's formation, a synoptic selection of main influences important to the current volume will be presented in Part I of this volume, specifically the archetypal approach of Dr. Henry Elkin (Elkin, 1972), Winnicott's *Human Nature* (1965, 1975, 1971, 1988), and Bion's *Transformations* (i.e., F and K in O, Bion, 1957, 1959). As will become evident in Parts I and II of this volume, Eigen's central notion of a *Sensitive Self* (2004) remains deeply informed by his unique *Elkin-Winnicott-Bion dialectic*. According to this dialectic, our autochthonous *being-in-the-world* is primarily informed (and transformed as radiant awakening) by our pristine ego's oceanic capacity, even if such worlding is initially proto-mental. The baby-mother of symbiosis and hatching follows our radiant awakening (as midwife unit to our "primordial consciousness"), in turn, to be followed by both the *baby-and-mother* of separation-individuation, as well as the triadic Oedipal drama as commencement to primordial Selfhood. Within these autochthonous epochs, if not archetypal dramas, self and Others are continually imbued with rich phantasy and imaginative potential, facilitating psychological growth and/or entropy within the *distinction–union trauma–nourishment dialectic*.

Eigen's writings, especially *Damaged Bonds* (Eigen, 2001a) and *Toxic Nourishment* (1999), describe a *Sensitive Self* (Eigen, 2004) laboring under too much or too little, suffering a poisoned mind–body–feeling self, necessitating psychic retreats, entombment, rigidity, and fusional softness as it attempts to survive nameless dread (Bion) and various primordial agonies (à la Winnicott). These works all serve as the *second ethnopoeinic* arch in Eigen's psychoanalytic writing. Poetically, Eigen states:

> Something goes wrong as personality begins to form, at the onset of self-organization, so that birth of self goes awry. One suffers distortion or is blown away. One tightens oneself to get through, but self-tightening creates distorted casings around distorted insides, hardening

and poisoning self. One holds vast areas of self at a distance, but poison spreads, and there is no safe haven. Winnicott speaks of two kinds of persons, one who does not carry around with them a significant experience of a mental break-down in earliest infancy and those who do. Those who do try to escape break-down with one foot and move toward it with the other. *Therapy provides a place to embrace this double movement and develop a better rhythm so that the breakdown-recovery movement can be fruitful.*

(2004, p. 23; emphasis added)

Reading Eigen, and held in all its infinite psycho-somatic variations and permutations, the loss of goodness in, and of the Other's ministration, serves as the foundation to not only the loss of primordial consciousness (in need of resurrection) but also to the primordial awakening of the destructive malevolent Other ("fear nucleus"). The *breakdown* (temporary or not) *recovery process* (partial or more than partially) relies on a merciful Other (as a rooting hormone) in countering annihilation anxieties and pressures, if not the commencement of the psychotic, semi-alive, damaged self and its mind-body splitting processes.[8] Registering and surviving toxic nourishment, if not holding and relating to what Eigen refers to as *primary process impacts* (Eigen, 1996), find the unfolding of archetypal and primordial rhythms needed for individuation. They may include birth–growth and damage–rebirth rhythms, trauma–nourishment rhythms, and healing longing in search of *faith rhythms*. The *rhythm of faith*, evident in Eigen's work since its inception, scaffolds union–distinction frustrations and traumas, enlivening the psyche's ability and need towards autochthonous unfolding. The rhythm of faith remains a central organizing psychoanalytic principle for Eigen, an ethical discipline, as well as loyal attitude in the psychoanalytic encounter (see Chapter 3).

Here I suggest that part of the rhythm Freud intuits has to do with a kind of psychic pulse, an opening–closing linked with *death–rebirth* (Elkin), *breakdown–recovery* (Winnicott), coming *alive–being murdered–feeling all right* (Bion) ... For Elkin one is born through a merciful Other after suffering boundless horror. For Winnicott trauma breaks personality as it forms, dread of breakdown persisting as an undercurrent associated with new beginnings ... For Bion it is as if one is murdered every time one tries to come alive.

(Eigen, 2004, pp. 33–34; emphasis added)

Furthermore, the primordial contact with a merciful (welcoming) Other is expected to *"interpenetrate, threaten, support, and feed emotional life"* (Eigen, 2004, p. 20). Each human psyche reflects a timeless interpenetrating self-other archive that limes the nascent self's continual struggle towards autochthonous expression. Such an archive holds the remnants of entropy and psychic dead spots, our deadening and hardening cores,[9] as well as each psyche's *inherent primal vitality* (Winnicott's I AM) and *sensitive self* potentiality. An analysand stated it as follows:

> I was rejected…I hardened myself, like a crab, hard shell, a too soft "inside." The soft inside feels too much, fears too much… It's the sensitivity that both haunts and supports me…to know the difference!

Another analysand:

> Constant conflict – my mind and thoughts are fractured. I cannot think – sensory mayhem, sensory chaos, pressure in my head, bursting – I cannot put anything together. I have to knock myself out with medication, re-boot myself.[10] This is linked to my *know-it-all* father and my *braindead* mom (Eigen's too much–too little). They are both unable to truly think me!

Eigen gives special attention and articulation to painful trauma artifacts, trauma clots, registers, signs, and signals – the "trauma globs" and "fright nucleus" (2001[11]) that remain in need of "transmutations" into "*useable* feeling/ imagining/thinking *flows*" (1995, p. 113; italics added), inherently serving as *guardian* to our damaged id, ego damage, and damaged unconscious.

> However, we also know, partly explicit in Freud, that the *unconscious, the psyche and the id can be damaged.*[12] They can be deranged, they can be damaged, and if they are damaged, the primary processes are unable to play a proper role in beginning to digest experience. The psyche remains in a state of perennial psychic indigestion. The primary process is important to help initiate digesting experience. And if it's damaged, it damages experience that it's trying to digest; it adds to the damage … *Tormented, tortured. A tortured psyche, a tortured unconscious.*
> (Eigen, 2019, p. 77; emphasis added)

To reiterate, the timeless interpenetration of the pristine and divine self–other (nourishment), as well as menacing self–other constellations (trauma globs, bad Other *as process*, tortured unconscious), serve as psychological soil to our psycho-spiritual growth (symbols), our capacity (or lack of) for soul care, as well as our damaged dream-work and the nourishment–trauma rhythms of our trauma registers (Eigen, 2019). Soul and psyche disaster can be micro-traumatic (Brandchaft, Doctors, and Sorter, 2010; Crastnopol, 2015; Kafka, 2017; Khan, 1963, 1972) even apocalyptic (Milner, 1969/2010), entombing and encapsulating the primordial Self (Eigen, 1986, Eshel, 2019). Various psychological adaptations, whether schizoid, psychopathic, or psychotic, reflect *desperate adaptations* to primordial traumas and will be evident in work to come on Elkin (Chapter 3) and Eigen's first analytic epoch (Chapter 4). That is, within Eigen's writing on the *Psychotic Core* (1986), the psychotic self, *Psychic Deadness* (1996), and trauma–nourishment (1999, 2001a), our sensitive self (2004, 2005) continuously struggles to deal with primordial injury, our *primordial broken-heartedness*. In an artful comparison between Judge Schreber and an analysand called Ruth (1986, chapter 7), Eigen maps primordial injury, mind–body madness (corrupt body self–corrupt mental self), epistemological reversal, omniscience, unintegration, the containerless container, the point of no return (primal aloneness), as well as therapeutic coordinates that can be relied upon to find a more meaningful, if not tolerable, relationship with self and others (see Eigen, 1986, pp. 306–312). The primordial disaster, the psyche's SOS (psychosis's primary language), finds a container worthy of transformation:

> In certain individuals, madness is obvious and the sense of unreality inescapable. In many others, it works silently; perhaps it is visible only in the gradual erosion of the quality of one's life and the deterioration of the capacity to generate vital and viable meaning.
>
> (Eigen, 1986, p. 331)

Silent or otherwise, Eigen's two case volumes, *Coming through the Whirlwind* (1992) and *Reshaping the Self* (1995), further support the reader to follow Eigen's holding of such "gradual erosion" processes as found in psychic dead spots, toxic nourishment, and damaged bonds. Bonds that wipe out sensitive self–other contact, impacting body-thinking-feeling-imagining-reverie-dreaming potential, leaving in its wake psychic scar tissue, emotional keloids, *thinking-feeling cachexia*, even uninhabitable psychological terrain. In Eigen's writing, both the visible and the not-so-visible psychological impacts are given their due. My analysands would describe Eigen's nourishment–trauma dialectic in words such as having to come to terms with various anti-growth experiences called "thought negatosis," "emotional rigor mortis," "being zombified," "a brain feeling botoxed," "thinking-feeling-digestive tract diverticulitis," "emotional black lung," and much more. Such injury to the primordial self could even see the cultivation of a deep-seated pessimism (Eigen's *cumulative injury rage*), malevolent transformations[13] found in narcissistic exoskeletons, and "faith"-less attitudes in the self and to the Other (even culture): "Cumulative rage helps nourish a pessimistic, depressive, semi-malevolent counter-part or undertow to one's official, happier self … chronic outrage over an injury can eat at life like an acid and corrode psychosomatic integrity" (1999, p. 48). Eigen mentions the possibility that *hydraulic and eliminative images*[14] may support and build capacity to make use of such injury-rage. However, psychosomatic and mental poisons are challenging to process. Embryonic equipment, if not faulty equipment, haunts our processing ability. Simultaneously, similar to radioactive wastelands, active distance and quarantine may at times be the only media available in allowing dispersal.

Further impact of self and others is explored in exquisite detail in the *third epoch* of Eigen's most personal writing: *Emotional Storm* (2005), *Rage* (2002), *Lust* (2006a), *Ecstasy* (2001), and *Feeling Matters* (2007). Similar to Bion's work on Love (L), Hate (H), Knowledge (K), and its inverse, -L, -H, -K links, Eigen probes religious, private, and public realities of our most profound storm kernels and affects. Being, growing, and learning in "bursts of lust" (2006a, p. 41), bursts of ecstasy, being and feeling enraged, finds Eigen breathing new life into areas so frequently, even in the act of psychoanalytic freedom, appropriated by superego discourse and cultural prohibitions and disdain.[15] A fascinating new lexicon is introduced for our collective psychic digestive systems, psychic skins, our power structures, and relational dilemmas, i.e., radioactive rage, rage radiation, rage as a cocoon of ache, radioactive breast-nipple-penis, educational rage, transformational rage, battle rage, domination rage, subservient rage, and much more. Emotional and imaginal sprouts (cuttings), with growth hormones added, reads into new possibilities – a most personal epoch in Eigen's analytic giving.

Following Eigen's third epoch writing, it becomes increasingly evident that the sensitive self's autochthonous strivings remain intimately engaged with various *cultural-spiritual strivings* (see Chapter 8). As such, Eigen's *fourth epoch* finds greater articulation and elaboration on themes such as evil, megalomania, mindlessness, omnipotence, spirituality, and human arrogance from within both an individual and collective perspective. That is, on both an interpersonal and cultural level, we may fail to serve as true psychic incubators for liberated futures, functioning predominantly as colonizers and instrumentalizers of self and others: a perennial deracinated and sensitive self dilemma projected onto various cultural artifacts, processes, and institutions. The dawn of the *Age of Psychopathy* (Eigen, 2006c) sees the severing of emotional nerves, election rape, mindless materialism – a growing collective soul ennui. Similar to Bion's concern about parasitic and symbiotic links in the container–contained, Eigen returns to soul wounding and the importance of the *area of faith*, the wisdom of the spiritual traditions in supporting our coming through *The Challenge of Being Human* (2018).

Finally, Eigen's *fifth epoch* of writing remains a beautiful testament in being human; cultivating a *rhythm of faith* able to serve as *seelsorge* to our trauma–nourishment realities, finding our own individual path (2016), sustaining our primordial soul needs for *Contact with the Depths* (2011) and *Faith* (2014), as well as surviving the flames of our passions and our unconscious. We, the agents of faith, the guardians to Freud's fear of soul entropy and activity gone wrong, are all in need of psychoanalytic *incubation*, allowing the possibility of a recovery-(re)growth capacity without having to solve perennial binds, endless Langian knots, or abort insoluble binds.

> At times, the best one can do is wait, let problems be, turn them over this way or that and see what happens in time. Waiting on a problem builds waiting ability. Tolerating difficulties builds tolerating ability…
>
> (Eigen, 2004, pp. 68–69)

> There are all kinds of ways to partly abort and partly go through rebirth processes. The *quality* of *coming through* is hampered by our human limitations, fragility, rigidity and "necessary" compromises with evil and madness, whether materialistic or idealistic.
>
> (Eigen, 2004, pp. 75–76)

Coming through activity gone wrong implies honestly meeting the wounding–obstructive–obdurate object, and our work remains embryonic. However, Eigen's decades-long work sees the possibility of developing psyche equipment and language, enabling our attempts at betterment; "I tend towards emphasizing helping someone come through a state, come through an experience. Going through, coming through, at least a little. A little can make a big difference." (Eigen, 2020, p. 124). Developing a psychic processor able to engage and work within a rhythm of faith does not aim at human perfection, discarding difficulty, or denying our human nature in the search for some soundproof sanity, as frequently seen in our contemporary preoccupation with normotic adjustment and calculative logic. In three thoughtful chapters titled "Soundproof Sanity" and "Fear of Madness" (in *Toxic Nourishment*, Eigen, 1999), as well as "Demons and Wounds" (Eigen, 2020, chapter 1), Eigen reflects: "But sanity is not a word I can handle right now, because there's so much hallucinated sanity, false sanity, sanitizing of destructive positions and pretending to be sane" (2020, p. 18). Normotic, developmentally induced, if not enforced socio-cultural alexithymia reminds of Joyce McDougal's *A Plea for a Measure of Abnormality* (1980).

Unfortunately, damaged bonds leave the psyche, in many ways, bereft of its inherent creativity as evident in being a sensitive and emotional self, its capacity for continuous rebirthing and recovering, frequently siding with Thanatos or the *anti-libidinal*. A further *fall out of doing over being* is the very psychic reality that we become deeply angered towards our inability and imperfections, our humanness as flawed and in need of mutual recognition and partnering (*anti-libidinal self*). Eigen again provides us with *psychological manna* in his writing,

> We punish ourselves for incapacity. A powerful force of self-rejection, in part, because we cannot do what we cannot do, a force in us that tries

to break through the intractable, tenuous ground in which life and death hang in the balance. In face of a massive self-destructive tendency, tolerance working with, appreciation of creative limits sounds better and better, if only it can be achieved. I remember how comforting it was to learn about the flaws in Asian rugs becoming a creative part of the pattern. And the more than comforting, vexing, inspiring ambiguity of flaws that grace, curse, and bless patterns of our lives with vicissitudes of possibility.

(Eigen, 2016, pp. 48–49)

For thoughts to come

As mentioned in the chapters to come, Eigen's own *sabbath point of the soul*, his most profound experiences that serve as *psychic genera*[16] à la Christopher Bollas (2011), will be explored through a rereading of Eigen's personal and professional experiences. Eigen leaves many psychoanalytic breadcrumbs for the reader, and I am confident every reader will find Eigen in their own unique and creative way. I envision Eigen, my innermost private Eigen, being content if every reader finds, refinds, and even redefines Eigen as they need or see fit. Given the latter, I will present a rather extensive network of themes as mentioned in my epoch-making statements. The epochs read primarily as linear and contextual and will include the (a) influence of Eigen's primary objects and early psychoanalytic interests, (b) the importance of Elkin, Winnicott, and Bion in constructing a rhythm of faith, (c) the various forces working against orphic potentiality, (d) sustaining faith in emotional storms and learning from affective experience, and (e) cultivating joy-based models to balance our reliance on mastery and control models. Early Eigen revisions Winnicottian thinking, for example, as a starting point to richer inner coordination, i.e., the psychic web-spinning that forecloses object usage and traps the subject in object relating or supports the narcotizing use of transitional objects (as a form of self-resistance). Developing psychological equipment to function as a primary process processor meeting catastrophe, cultivating a radical openness in the distinction–union dialectic, being able to ignite dreaming the undreamble murderous superego that traps the T-ego and body–ego dialectic (see Chapter 3), developing an alimentary system (T-ego and body-ego types) able to detoxify the tragedy of toxic nourishment as received in damaged bonds, all remain psychological achievements and are modulated by our inherent transcendental capacity (primordial Self capacity), the presence of a merciful Other, and our ever-growing capacity for object usage. A deeply traumatized schizo-affective analysand reflected on the latter as follows:

> Even in all the bad that happened to me with people, I have experienced some good, some good moments, *with* and *in* them. Even with God's torment of my small being, His wanting to destroy me with fire… there is

something greater than those spirits, *more than even them*. Even in me, there is more; there is something *behind* all this, *something there. Deep within.*

Eigen's writing remains in its essence a hopeful, creative testament of our inherent "more," even if injured, our capacity to experience ourselves and others with feeling, and that our *feelings do, in fact, matter*. Eigen's psychotic core and sensitive self are "active" remnants of the various factors and forces that try to undo and reverse our forward-moving capacities. By *partnering* with such forces we may be able to find our once-in-a-lifetime path, working creatively with our *"self-resistance"* (2016, p. 8) in *agony X* and Winnicott's +z realities. But first, Eigen's own primal background of experience as foundation to his ontological psychoanalysis.

Notes

1 The title of this chapter is taken from an article published by Eigen (2008) in *Psychoanalytic Dialogues.*
2 Eigen's article *The Personal and Anonymous 'I'* (in Gibson, Lathrop, & Stern, 1986) remains a testament to the creative and generative unconscious.
3 For a detailed reading of Eigen's *own reflections* of major writing themes 1973–1989, please refer to the *Afterword* in the *Electrified Tightrope* (1993, pp. 259–278).
4 For detailed clinical reading on Eigen's *rebirth model* see *Coming through the Whirlwind* (1992), and Eigen in Fuchsman and Cohen (2021, chapter 1).
5 Review Eigen's *dosaging* concept, in *Psychic Deadness* (1996).
6 I use the symbol to articulate the eternal inter-relationship evident in Eigen's trauma–nourishment dialectic.
7 "At the beginning," Winnicott (1965, p. 84) wrote, similar to Eigen's distinction–union dialectic, "the infant is entirely dependent on the physical provision of the live mother and her womb or her infant care. But in terms of psychology we have to say that the infant is *at one and the same time dependent and independent. It is this paradox that we need to examine.*" (Italics added.)
8 See Eigen's *Psychotic Self* concept, chapter 8, in *The Psychotic Core* (1986).
9 See *"I am turning into a barnacle"*, in *Dialogues with Michael Eigen* (2020, chapter 11).
10 Also see Eigen's case of Dolores, chapter 5, in the *Psychoanalytic Mystic* (1998), as well as *The Stinging Nipple* in *Rage* (2002, pp. 91–99).
11 See *Damaged Bonds*, 2001, pp. 24–28, calling forth Archetypal Defenses (Kalsched, 1996, 2013).
12 See especially *Damaged Bonds*, chapters 1–4.
13 'Mischievous, Malignant Rage,' in *Rage*, Eigen (2002, pp. 116–123).
14 Also review Eigen's "Reflections on eating and breathing as models of mental functions," *American Journal of Psychoanalysis*, 41 (1981): 177–180.
15 See the cases of *Lily*, Eigen (2006, pp. 52–55); *Soren*, Eigen (2002, pp. 17–20); and *Fred*, Eigen (2002, pp. 40–44) for clinical elaborations of Eigen's third epoch writing.
16 See Bollas (2011, chapter 5, pp. 57–78), especially pp. 70–71 titled "Steps in the formation of genera."

Chapter 2

The primal background of experience

Eigen and his primary imaginal Others

> Adults in my life were sensitive and feeling. Affect was in the air. But it was not a sensitivity or feeling that makes a child's feelings visible or palpable. It was feeling and sensitivity unto itself, atmospheric ... It was a sort of emotional atmosphere without a sense of a child's subjectivity. The result felt like two trees in the middle of my garden, one without nerve-endings, the other with a rich supply of nerve endings and, with Schreber, soul was in the nerves.
>
> (Eigen, 2007, p. 91)

On living with mother and father

Eigen writes in the afterword in the *Electrified Tightrope* (1993, pp. 259–278) of two major developmental epochs, i.e., living *without* (first 18 years of his life)[1] and living *with* psychoanalysis. Eigen's writing strives to bring into meaningful dialogue his pre-analytic, extra-analytic, and psychoanalytic self (selves?) in all of his written work. Eigen's primordial background of experience, surviving an immigrant environment where pain was taken for granted, and sojourns into psychoanalysis serve as psychic lifeblood throughout countless book volumes.

Michael Eigen was born in Passaic, New Jersey, more than 80 years ago to Jeanette (née Brody) and Sol Eigen. His mother was a teacher, and his father a self-made businessman and lawyer. According to Eigen:

> In Passaic I learned the value of immersion in everyday experience. This meant immersion in painful as well as pleasurable realities, painful-pleasurable struggles with peers, parents, and society. Sometimes, unexpectedly, spontaneous moments of absolute joy emerged from immersion in mixed realities. One such moment was seeing the stars when *I was little over 2*, a moment that has never left me. *The shock of awe-filled joy was definitive*. Another was the way I felt after kissing a girl I loved when I was 16 or 17. I danced and sang all the way home – all-stars. The kind of joy

DOI: 10.4324/9781003002871-3

is an elemental given, reduceable to nothing. If anything other than itself
at all, it is a song of God.

(1993, p. 259)

Reading Eigen's earliest memories and experiences reminds me of Eigen,
the later psychoanalytic writer.[2] An inherent sensitivity to experience a kind
of joyous self-world-visual-mouth-body-God kiss, irreducible shock-awe
experiences that enliven Eigen to ecstasy in mixed realities. With an apparent
openness and innate capacity for joy and bliss, Eigen naturally experienced
the opposite: "The loneliness and isolation of my first five years remain a persistent part of me. I longed for friends" (1993, p. 261). According to Eigen
(1993), his longing and loneliness served as a creative impetus to becoming
a writer; that is, writing is to share, connect, and remain. Being-with, being-
without, joy, ecstasy, and loneliness are central themes for Eigen, and prepare
for various later concepts such as his distinction–union dialectic.[3] Eigen freely
mentions many such childhood moments in his work, reflective of a preco-
ciousness and an ability to retain something of a "sense of holiness," if not
wonder; a head-heart capacity he would much later call in his own body-work
his *vaginal heart,*

> Heaven keeps opening. Invagination is often an implied image. In my
> early twenties, after a physical intervention by a somatic therapist, he
> asked how I felt, and I spoke the truth, "I feel like a vagina." My whole
> body became vaginal. His [body therapist] paranoid aspect came to the
> fore and said, How do you know how a vagina feels?" At that moment,
> in my experience, I was one. A vaginal self, a vaginal body. A Lacanian
> might say imaginary vagina.
>
> (Eigen, 2014, p. 77)[4]

Openness and joy for Eigen are also found in other "*elemental areas of
experience*" (1993, p. 260), most notably religion, music, and sports. Faith,
harmony, and physical play deeply informed and supported Eigen's body-
sensing, his connecting to others, allowing his psyche to sing. Most notable,
concerning faith, Eigen writes on meeting Rabbi Kellner and being impacted
by his radiant face,[5] areas Eigen creatively later explore as a psychoanalyst;

> I remember the light that came from his face. It took many years for
> me to begin to grasp the *stirring I felt in his presence was a sense of
> holiness.* I am thankful this sense survives my life, uplifts me as an ana-
> lytic person, and ignites sessions. *It may easily have died in suffering and
> sophistication.*
>
> (Eigen, 1993, p. 260; emphasis added)

Rabbi Kellner, who had a face unlike any other. A kindly, intelligent, human face that made you quiver, thaw, which lifted you.

(Eigen, 2007, p. 77)

Given an inherent soul sensitivity, living from his soul garden he naturally sees the presence of various trauma–nourishment seeds, the primordial reality of maternal and paternal impacts:

GOVRIN: In one of your books you describe how much your mother hurt you when you were a baby.

EIGEN: My mother was supportive and caring. Nevertheless, I felt terribly hurt by her going to work when I was very young, about eight months old. Child-caring thrilled, frightened, and stifled her. She needed to get out of the house to be herself another way ... There is more I am afraid to say because it sounds crazy or impossible. I still feel the *rip* of her leaving to go to work when I was eight months old. The feeling that she couldn't (didn't want to) be with me and had to get away, the suffocated feeling she was escaping, and the *tear through my body*. My bearing it, *hardening, making do*. I learned to tell time in my crib, putting together the hands of the clock[6] in my field of vision with morning radio shows ... I remember – or imagine I remember – the eureka of matrices coming together and realizing the time the talk show host announced dove-tailed with the position of the hands and numbers of the clock ... The visual sight with the radio voice ...

GOVRIN: Why were you so preoccupied with the clock at that age?

EIGEN: It was a *recurrence, a correlation, a connection.* Clock, radio, mother's leaving and returning – all parts of an affective spatial-temporal emotional, cognitive field that clicked together. I suppose the radio voice was a kind of mother. *You piece together what you can with materials at hand.* Radio was part of my life until I left for college. Later, as a teen, I listened to jazz when I went to sleep, and the jazz host told the time. Now I listen to news a lot and classical music. *Still mothering myself, not always in good ways.*

(Eigen, 2007, pp. 85–86; emphasis added)

Eigen's mother was born on the Lower East Side of New York City, her parents from Poland, and of Jewish heritage. Eigen describes his mother as patient, athletic, intelligent, able to enjoy her independence, persistent, softer than his father, and steady. Outbursts were rare. As just mentioned, child-caring thrilled, frightened, and stifled Eigen's mother, and Eigen remained deeply sensitive to his mother's need to be outside the house. Eigen also writes of not liking her food, a symbol of both her care and lack; "I understood at the time my feeling about her food was also about her. Goodness was there, caring was there, reliability was there, but something was missing" (2007, p. 84). Eigen's sensitivity meant being able to hold, if not steel (hardening) himself from his mother's distance, describing the awareness as follows, "I can feel the contraction, a stiffening, as well as a sobbing inside that goes on and on" (2007, p. 85), only later to be called a sour puss, rather than being partnered as a *sensitive self*. It may also be evident that this sensitivity to his mother's need to be "away" may have stimulated a precocity to protect against the absent mother's[7] inability to comprehend his *psycho-spiritual makeup*; "I don't think my mother could experience my tormented nature, or maybe she did not know what to do with such agonized awareness" (2007, p. 90). Eigen's mother was undoubtedly aware of his emotional needs, although in more "global, non-specific ways" (2007, p. 90).

To add further pain and confusion to maternal distance, Eigen mentions being left in the care of a babysitter experienced as "crazily scary" (2007, p. 88), combined with the reality "that I was not listened to about her added to my sense of isolation. Helpless fear, rage, clotted bad feeling, sick feeling. I had a deep sense of not being taken seriously, in spite of their care and devotion and love" (2007, p. 89). For Eigen, being listened to, being taken seriously, and implicitly believed became a psychological imperative, if not a reparative drive in later psychoanalytic writing. Eigen struggled with both presence and absence, and in many works (i.e., *Toxic Nourishment,* 1999, and *Damaged Bonds,* 2001, especially) returns to types of parenting and their *impacts*. Bearing a child's emotional difficulty and difference remains a challenge for most parents. It is not infrequent to talk, wish, push, force, or threaten a child's emotional difficulties away. Despite loneliness and absence, and similar to Sabina Spielrein and many others, Eigen clearly possessed the *wise baby* complex and remained a primary process lover. We are indeed fortunate for this ability.

Concerning early paternal influences[8] (grandfather and father), Eigen describes his father as anxious, overprotective, rageful – a parental love that "squelched, compressed, deformed me. I think a part of my energy involves a wish to be free, push past confines, burst through a sense of being held back" (2007, p. 76). Although, as with mother, there was undoubtedly love and warmth, Eigen mentions a lack of psychological understanding, "not what Winnicott called *percipience*" (2007, p. 76; emphasis added) and, "He didn't really know who I was, didn't know me. I was a picture in his mind, an appendage of his ego" (2007, p. 76). Eigen came to understand, in time, the impact of his father's own early losses that cemented a "good heart-good deed" approach to life, an approach "not attuned to possibilities of intersubjective affective transmissions; damage affective attitudes transmit from insides to insides" (2007, p. 78). Unable to access genuine affective intersubjectivity, Eigen's unique soul needs and sensitivities remained neglected.

In a later conversation with Aner Govrin (2007), two crucial and analytically rich *grandfather provisions* are discussed, further illustrating the painful misattunement between the paternal and Eigen. Eigen mentions that, although his grandfather owned a candy store, a young child's dream, Eigen's grandfather would paradoxically provide Eigen with Indian nuts instead. Not only was Eigen's desire left unfulfilled, but Eigen was exposed to an added burden of struggle – cracking the Indian nuts, something Eigen's grandfather had no difficulty in achieving. To Eigen, it was as if his grandfather gave him "practice [in] meeting challenges, *work hard at getting nourishment* ... Hard nuts,[9] tiny eatable insides in tough and difficult shells ... Trauma tough, crazy sensitive insides pushing into life, looking into corners with fear ... Life as hard and nutty ... A casual enactment, demonstrating the precision of unconscious transmission in everyday life. Now I see hardening and cracking magnified in the world at large" (2007, pp. 78–79). With this magnified hardening (the paternal lineage as with mother), Eigen's grandfather also introduced a "sliver of joy," in purchasing a much wished-for silver police whistle – a prized object Eigen could rely on to stop the world. "Blowing a silver whistle, stopping the world. But life went on as usual except I had a sliver of silver joy, a sense of getting lucky in a sea of frustration" (2007, p. 78).

Finally, Eigen's father also provided other distal, although vital gifts: being self-made, a strong work ethic, surviving anti-Semitic trauma, a love for the law – not so much its practice as it is infrequently applied ethically[10] – playing chess, and being a family man. Eigen, the psychoanalyst, would frequently return to these parental patterns in various trauma statements, accentuating the reality that parents disturb their children just as children disturb their parents – a mutual disturbance in need of its own evolutionary process. Parental personality can inflict damage: psychic concussion, lacerations, irritations, and inflammation. But reparation and closeness may become possible in time. Having to push beyond hard and hardening beginnings, constant struggle, and "steeling" oneself has many implications and creative possibilities. These developmental and lived themes are creatively scattered through nearly 30 volumes of work.

On Henry Elkin: Eigen's living Socrates

Henry Elkin,[11] Eigen's Socrates, undoubtedly played a pivotal role in Eigen's life. As the reader will soon discover, Elkin remains a creative and seminal part in various of Eigen's concepts and clinical sensibilities. Eigen consulted Dr. Elkin at the tender age of 21 and described Elkin as having more self-possession with "a resonant voice reverberating echoes of the psyche ... When I met Henry I felt the reality of the breathing psyche" (2016, pp. 6–7). According to Eigen, Elkin trained at the Zurich Institute as a Jungian psychoanalyst, where Emma Jung served as his training analyst. During the first year of therapy, Eigen decided to travel after being motivated by Jack Kerouac's work *On the Road*. Eigen did not return for some time to analysis with Elkin and, after taking a course with Rollo May at the New School for Social Research, returned to Elkin on May's recommendation. Eigen remained in full-time analysis from 1960–1968, during which time Eigen was exposed to, and was part of, an evolving Elkin. Being an open, contemporary, and creative thinker, Elkin abhorred isolationism, group conflict, intellectual minimalism as "From the beginning, he wanted to bring together positive findings of depth psychologies into a comprehensive framework ... He was sensitive to the significance of the moment and the times" (2016, p. 5). Therapeutic scarring did take place, as Eigen mentions he felt "devastated" when Elkin "abruptly" left New York after the breakup of his marriage and accepting a professorship at Duquesne University. Elkin supported Eigen in finding another therapist, a child therapist, Dorothy Bloch, and Eigen stayed with her for two years, "I got what I needed and am grateful to her" (2016, p. 5; emphasis added):

> My analysis with Henry ended without a promise fulfilled. There were terrible feelings I came to him with that he felt analysis would help. In this respect, the analysis was a broken promise. *In fact, the analysis did something unexpected. It did not "cure" the ill I came with but added much to my capacity to be that I could not anticipate. I was more than I was, although a sick self remained.* I often tell a patient who wants to know if the bad feeling will ever leave, "It may or may not, but it will take up less room."

Eigen poignantly mentions that, although both analysts contributed in various ways, a "deep ill-feeling did not leave until my seventies" (2016, p. 6). Despite such "deep ill-feeling," Eigen writes that "one offshoot" of his work with Elkin was becoming a psychotherapist. Attending both individual and group therapy with Elkin enabled Eigen, then mainly doing teaching jobs, to accept work at a school for disturbed children. Elkin introduced Eigen to Mira Rothenberg, the head of Blueberry, a treatment center and camp for schizophrenic children, "Without realizing it, this was a turning point. Mira was rich with psyche and practical wisdom and supported me in using everything I had. It was a true gift, digging deeply into oneself to find a way of helping another" (2016, p. 6). Elkin also supported Eigen to enter graduate school at age 27, achieving his doctorate within six years and publishing psychoanalytic works internationally! Despite many psychological gifts and immeasurable emotional-spiritual development, Eigen acknowledges that Elkin's limitations, especially his relationship with women, necessitated further separate psychological work. Sessions with Wilfred Bion, André Green, and Michael Kriegsfeld enabled Eigen to achieve marriage and raise a family, a deep soul need for Eigen. Eigen also humbly reflects on the various analysts and colleagues that supported his psychic growth, the importance of the psychoanalytic milieu *per se* as creative container, his learning from various analysands, and the impact of his family wounds and trauma on his career choice. All combine as background support to inner evolution.

> I stayed with my patients longer than my analyst stayed with me. I was trying to complete my analysis and heal myself through them. My analytic work was motivated by my need to repair my own broken analysis. It was, too, trying to mend the unmendable. My younger brother was killed by a truck when he was almost 11 and I was 21. My mother never fully recovered, and to say I felt guilty does not even come close. *I suspect I became an analyst in part to bring my brother back to life.* This is one reason why I have been attracted to the impossible and worked so long with many given up on by others – the *psychotic* (*The Psychotic Core*, 1986), the *unwanted, undeveloped, malignant, recalcitrant,* or otherwise *maimed self* (*The Electrified Tightrope*, 1993), the *dead* (*Psychic Deadness*, 1996).
>
> (Eigen, 2001a, p. 162)

Eigen and Bion: dreaming, marriage, and getting on with the nasty business of finding *and* being oneself

Eigen met Bion in 1978 in New York. In many of Eigen's writings, the reader meets a Bion that supported, if not allowed Eigen, to follow a deep heart desire, that is, to move from psychoanalysis to marriage and fatherhood.[12] Bion's unique and sensitive alertness to *nurturing difference* "woke me up, presented it in a way that I could hear, in a way that got through to me … pushed me into *birthing myself even more* … to go beyond my current life … trying to help me into life" (2007, pp. 33–34; emphasis added), helpfully describing marriage to Eigen as follows; "It's just two people speaking truth to one another, a relationship to help mitigate the severity to yourself" (2007, p. 32). Even more poignantly, "Bion was a spokesperson for an inner voice in my youth. I had long wanted to marry and be a father. But I wanted many other things and became absorbed in my analysis instead of marrying" (1999, p. 217). Bion's own sensitivity to *wanting to be*, if not being *different*, made him "alert to nurturing difference" (2007, p. 35), exquisitely in tune with the complexities and mixed realities concerning "the nasty business of finding oneself" (2007, p. 36). Furthermore, Eigen candidly mentions in *Ecstasy* (2001b, pp. 71–72) that he even told Bion he found him joyless![13] With "reflective immediacy" (p. 71), Bion responded, "Then you must realize joy in your body, all through you. It must shine in your skin." (2001b, p. 71). As Bion clearly understood, since essential to Eigen, joy must reverberate and shine through senses, muscle, skin, and pores. A stunning moment of Bion's *alpha functioning in vivo*, sensing Eigen's need and nature in real time. Impact. Contact. Being met. Finally, Eigen also reflects on the unique ebb and flow of their connection, their psyche-to-psyche interaction, Bion's waiting capacity in awakening psychic truth, not just in the meeting but even in *Eigen's use of writing as making contact years later*,

> We drifted on, and I, finally, feeling guilty, would begin to go. That is my nature. I break contact too quickly. I think of the way he stood there waiting for me, chatting on, whenever I ended a session quickly. He left time open for a slower ending or continuation. To be able to wait for each other- such a valuable trait. How many of us can do this or want to most of the time?
>
> (Eigen, 2001b, p. 71)

Waiting for beginnings and *beginning to wait* (see Eigen, 2020, chapter 6) remains central to Eigen's Bion.

Eigen and André Green: on protecting object relations in an area of faith

Eigen met André Green a year after his sessions with Bion.[14] For Eigen, Green was an enlivening analyst with creativity and imagination, especially allowing psychosis to come out of the closet (think too of Bion's psychotic part of the personality). As a student of Bion, Winnicott, and Lacan, Green seemed a natural fit to Eigen's sensibilities and psychoanalytic concerns. At least from reading Eigen's account of their first meeting, a unique psychoanalytic distinction–union experience seemed intrinsically operative.[15] By the mid-1970s, both analysts had cultivated a core sensitivity to the double anxieties (abandonment–intrusion) evident in the distinction–union dialectic. It is also of interest to read Eigen's wholehearted confrontation of Green, accusing him of "stealing" his work; "I knew my suspicion that he was pilfering my stuff was nutty, but let it all hang out." (2007, p. 38).[16] Green was experienced by Eigen as firm, holding, non-reactive, allowing for an unfolding of Eigen's soul concerns. The link between Bion's comments on marriage and Eigen's discussion of a dream with Green remains astounding, a testament to how Eigen held, in time and space, a central concern between his analysts. In this dream,[17] Eigen envisions a lovely woman, but made less so, due to her problematic eyes (something 'wrong' with her eyes):

EIGEN: I interpreted that this woman lacks something with regards to consciousness.

GREEN: It's your dream, and your aggression created this image, marring her, seeing her in a negative light.

(2007, p. 38)

Given the transference, Green interpreted that the difficulty was Eigen's *own eyes*, his fear of marrying the love object; thus, his eyes are finding defects to dismiss the object that is loved, "seeing faults to justify fleeing" (2007, p. 38, as with Bion and "breaking contact"). Green's reading and holding of Eigen's inner need and dilemma had a profound effect on Eigen, and as with Bion, supported Eigen in moving closer to his heart's desire (although Eigen admits to further work with another therapist over a few years),

> Three therapists teamed up (British, French, and American) to finally get me across the line. It took a lot to link up with myself and do what I long felt I wanted … Green saved the dream from me, from a destructive way of seeing. He protected my psyche from me. … He did it deftly, firmly, light of touch, clearly. *He was protecting a link with life from attacks on it*. The object – Green, my wife-to-be, my psyche – survived my attacking aspect. A kind of *use of object* (Winnicott) situation: the other surviving destruction becomes more fully other, someone one can be with.
>
> (Eigen, 2007, pp. 38–39; emphasis added)

Eigen on Winnicott: spontaneous recognition of the other as inherently valued, being allowed to be off-center, and object survival

Ten years before consulting Bion, Eigen met with Winnicott in 1968, "At the time I was near a dramatic end of eight years of analysis" (2007, p. 40). Eigen writes in various book volumes about being touched by Winnicott's spontaneous, respectful treatment and his general openness to Eigen and his ideas. A profound psychoanalytic generosity and respect were evident. As an Eigen reader, I was struck by the case discussion that transpired between Eigen and Winnicott. Winnicott presented Eigen with an artistic description of a rather unusual request by a female analysand. In this request, Winnicott was to sit behind the analysand, and in doing so, would allow the analysand to position/ center Winnicott's face in the analysand's own hand-held mirror. Winnicott became aware that his face seemed somewhat off-center, and as such, moved to center his image as a gesture of support, even "help" (2007, p. 41). The analysand mentioned to Winnicott that if he had done this very "support" six months previously, rehospitalization would have been necessary! Eigen reflects:

> In trying to help her get it right, he was like her mother, unable to tolerate not being the perfect center of her mind. I was left with a sense of the importance of learning to tolerate being off-balance, off-kilter, off-center. Even being dangled and tantalized by another without loss of patience, faith, and skill.
>
> (2007, p. 41)

As with meeting other psychoanalytic giants (Bion and Green), all stood for not overpowering the other, that is, unduly pressurizing an analysand's inner working, or bringing thinking-feeling-being to premature foreclosure. Winnicott's narration also stands as a verbal testament to our immense sensitivity when considering psychological survival when *viewed* by the other, even if *we* are holding the mirror. Eigen also wrote feeling touched as an 'unknown' psychoanalyst asked by Winnicott if he should present his ideas at the New York Psychoanalytic Society; specifically, his now highly acclaimed "Use of the object" paper (Winnicott, 1969). It is well known that Winnicott was met with much hostility, was "butchered,'" and suffered a heart attack the very evening of his presentation (Eigen, 2007, p. 42). From destructive inner eyes to the establishment's own critical "optic rectomitis": attacks that butcher, kill, or attempt to kill internal needs, creativity, links, ideas, and being with each other, even when off-center. Psychoanalytic creativity can be dangerous, subject to destructive attacks, murdering the feeling-heart. New York analytic could not creatively *hold* being off-kilter or what seemed off-kilter.

Despite such tragedy, Eigen mentions further gifts that nourished his own being as related to Winnicott, "I saw his awkward intensity and thought, 'He is like me. It's alright to be the kind of person I am. He was giving me permission to be myself, so much as I dared'" (1986, p. 86). Paired with such lived permission in and of being oneself, Eigen writes in *Faith* (2014b, chapter 3) that reading Winnicott provided him with a similar profound sense of *psyche relief and freedom*. Winnicott's writing and style created for Eigen an "atmospheric background," (2014b, p. 23) wherein "I could breath more freely with Winnicott, with myself, my patients, more readily take people as they are without demeaning judgments, stay with what is, opening fields of experience" (2014b, p. 24). In essence, Elkin-Bion-Green-Winnicott all remain unique symbols of neonic freedom for Eigen and his ontological work to come.

Notes

1 Also see chapter 10, "Some biographical notes," in Eigen's 2016 book titled *Image, Sense, Infinities, and Everyday Life*. I rely here on Dr. Eigen's own description as written in *The Electrified Tightrope* (1993), p. 259.

2 For a close reading see the character Smith in *On Demonized Aspects of the Self* in *The Electrified Tightrope* (1993, chapter 16) and *Psychic Deadness,* chapter 9, titled *The Counterpart* (1996).

3 See chapter 7, "Alone points," in *Feeling Matters* (2007) and chapter 1 in *Kabbalah and Psychoanalysis* (2012).

4 For an in depth reading see Eigen's *Faith* (2014b), chapter 7, entitled "Variants of mystical participation."

5 See also chapters 6 through 9 in the *Electrified Tightrope* (1993) for an in-depth discussion on the significance of the face.

6 Clock symbolism is described by Sabina Spielrein and can be found in the Appendix of her article "Contributions to understanding a child's mind" (1913) in Spielrein (2019, chapter 3).

7 For a beautiful psyche moment between Dr. Eigen and his mother see "The pain machine," pp. 128–130, in the *Psychoanalytic Mystic* (1998).

8 Also see, for a synoptic read, *Dialogues with Eigen: Psyche Singing* (2020), chapter 17, "In the land of the unknown," pp. 230–238.

9 Eigen's sensitivity to softness-hardness is creatively explored in chapter 10, *The Electrified Tightrope* (1993, pp. 105–108).

10 Eigen adds a spiritual dimension to his Father in *Ecstasy* (2001b), pp. 92–93.

11 Eigen writes (in Daws, 2016, pp. 5–6); "From 1960–68 we worked at first five, then four and finally three times a week. My work with Dorothy was once a week from beginning to end. I felt palpable relief the first session. As I was leaving I asked if she thought I could be helped. She replied, 'We can only try.' Before I closed the door she added, 'Have a good week.' Within a year, I began to feel good, a gift cherished till this moment, *although the deep ill-feeling did not leave until my seventies*, long after Henry and Dorothy passed away."

12 Bion's response to Eigen to "stop analysis" and enter marriage also included an important message to psychoanalysts: "Transference is enriching but also potentially enslaving" (2007, p. 33).

13 "He [Bion] still was formal, somewhat stiff, measured, yet friendly, forthcoming, welcoming. Not in that easygoing, informal American way. He had a professional aura. But you felt he was tuned in, listening to something – a psychic bearing. That is, his formality and stiffness was not simply social manners but a kind of *psychic sentience. A bird has a sort of stiffness, but it is alert and sensing.*" (Eigen, 2007, p. 35). I cannot help but think of the framed seagull picture in Dr. Eigen's office behind his chair.

14 Also see "My session with André", chapter 7, in Eigen (2016).

15 See Eigen in Govrin (2007, pp. 36–38).

16 I am reminded here of Eigen's Winnicottian thinking as read in the "Area of faith" article: "The infant goes all out at the object and the latter must see to it that it survives" (1993, p. 116).

17 Also review "Encounters: Bion, Green, Winnicott" (in 2007, pp. 32–43) wherein Eigen discusses Bion's thinking on the dream (p. 35). For further study on Eigen and the use of his own dreams and dreaming see Eigen (2005, chapter 6).

Chapter 3

Eigen's area of faith

Prominent theorists as background support

> By the area of faith I mean to *point to a way of experiencing* that is undertaken with one's whole being, all-out, 'with all one's heart, with all one's soul, and with all one's might.'
>
> (Eigen, 1993, p. 109)

Introduction

Various theorists played pivotal roles in Eigen's creative psychoanalytic vision. Eigen writes throughout his indebtedness to S. Freud, C. Jung, H. Elkin, M. Klein, H. Kohut, P. Federn, M. Milner, D. W. Winnicott, and M. Khan, to name but a few.[1] Seminal Eigen articles and book chapters, such as "The area of faith in Winnicott, Lacan, and Bion"[2] (1993, chapter 11), as well as "Rhythm of faith" (2004, chapter 2), find Eigen focusing and expanding, most specifically, on the work of Wilfred Bion, D. W. Winnicott, and Henry Elkin. Given the introductory nature of the current volume, Eigen's theoretical triptych will serve as the primary, albeit limited, theoretical orientation.

Elkin's ontology of self

Elkin's theoretical perspective on the *Ontology and Origin of Self* reflects timeless Jungian insights into the human infant's primordial dramas. Detailed expositions on "clinical and theoretical Elkin" can be found throughout many of Eigen's works, especially *The Psychotic Core* (1986) and *The Sensitive Self* (Eigen, 2004). In particular, two seminal papers, "On the origin of the self" (1958) and "On selfhood and the development of ego structures in infancy" (1972), serve as psychological soil for many of Eigen's micro-sensitivities[3] and should be studied in depth, with Bion and Winnicott, as Eigen's seminal soul ontology triptych.

DOI: 10.4324/9781003002871-4

Elkin's ontogenetic origin of the self

Elkin's theory on the *Ontogenetic Origin of the Self* creatively conceptualizes a primordial "I" predating an awareness of a "body I" or "conceptual I" (i.e., "a primordial I/Self," Sartre's *existence precedes essence*). Elkin's psychoanalytic approach, in essence, posits that the primordial Self and its consciousness[4] can be found in the earliest mother–infant moments of contact, *earlier* than the initially held notion that "the ego is first and foremost body ego." As articulated by Eigen in *The Psychotic Core* (1986), and subsequently returned to in most of his later works (especially *The Sensitive Self*, 2004, and *Emotional Storm*, 2005), Elkin's initial anthropological task was to pose the following question, "What kind of world does the infant live in if he is aware of self-other before he knows he has a body?" For the Freudian baby, given its biological–instinctual needs, the ego is, first and foremost, a body-ego. Elkin, in contrast, postulates a primordial "awareness" and "consciousness" that predates the accepted Freudian logic and articulates a Self subject to four main stages of infantile development:[5]

(1) *Birth to three months*, characterized by a *collective-erotic sensing* (ontogenetic preconsciousness). This developmental period predates the smiling response and remains reliant on the instinctual reactions of *attraction and repulsion*. Primordial affects, connected with the instinctual reactions of attraction–repulsion, are pre-self-conscious and are closely linked to fear, need, and rage.

(2) *Three to six months*, principally the primordial Objects' domain (Elkin, 1972), wherein the primordial Self-*and*-Other "awareness" blossoms. The "self" is experienced as distinct from non-self. However, all sensory experience remains is global, all-encompassing, and increasingly under the sway of *mental-spiritual-physical growth* and its resulting *"primordial drama."* Need begets self-experience, response, and the evocation of the Other. The primordial Other, through co-union, brings either bliss or terror, similar to Winnicott's *Z* dimension to be discussed shortly. *Mental-spiritual death-resurrection*[6] moments are *the* earliest memory traces of the Other and the basis of time, spatiality, *coming-into-being-with,* and *coming-through* (see Eigen's *crib mind*). Eigen's writing in the *Psychotic Core* (1986), especially his concept of the *Psychotic Self* (1986, chapter 8), explores this development area in much creative detail.

(3) *Six to eight months*, a transitional period in which the primordial Self encompasses the physical body and thus the grammar of the instinctual self and "dangerous and the good Other." Archetypically, this is the domain of the Good and Evil Mother. A cosmic struggle wherein holy rage turns to hate and physical destruction of the frustrating other, à

la Melanie Klein, wins over annihilation of self (mental-spiritual death). Good enough parenting (Elkin's *merciful love*) allows for identification and survival of the Good Mother, development of guilt.

(4) *Eight months onwards*, wherein the infant's relationship to embodiment and its ever-growing world-self-other capacity allows for greater integration between what Elkin called the transcendental or mind-ego (T-ego) and the body-ego demands.

Before a general Elkin journey is attempted, it may prove beneficial to review Elkin's view of the ego (T and body ego structures) as Eigen thickens Elkin's thinking on the ego throughout his many works. For Elkin, although the infant is linked to the mother concretely and directly by virtue of breastfeeding and holding, infants not only nurse (mouth-nipple connection, body-ego states) but also continuously *gaze*[7] at the mother's breast and face. Developmentally, as argued by Elkin, the primordial ego is initially an "eye-mind" to be followed by six months with the infant's growing awareness of having a mouth connected to the "breast," to the mother as a physical entity, and thus the creation of a "mouth/body-mind."[8] In Elkin's logic, the latter follows Freud's instinctual development and is part of the body-ego. Whereas the *eye-mind* serves as the transcendental ego or *T-ego, the body-ego, in contrast, given the direct link with the maternal, falls under the sway of maternal ministrations (natural values) and her so-called goodness-badness.* The body-ego reflects the shift from the child being a "child of God" to the *world of the Mother and later the Father*. Spiritual values (T-ego) meet material worlding (body-ego). The mother also functions as a mediator between the primordial and the human worlds (as archetypal mediatrix). Although the mediation processes become increasingly complex in the transitional phase of development as characterized by both Winnicott and Eigen, for Elkin, an *area of the ego* remains forever part of the cosmic struggle against the Evil Mother, that is, less identified with body-ego identification than with the original mental-spiritual sovereignty of the Good Mother, the original facial expressions tracing back to the primordial T-ego experience with (M)Other. It is expected, however, that by the end of the eighth month of development, the child will recognize that the Good Mother and the Evil Mother[9] are the same person, casting the *T-ego* into confusion, inhibiting through fear the body-ego's freedom to express its instinctual intensities (fury) against the (M)Other.

To return to Elkin's developmental schema, in the *primordial* stage of individual life, "the new-born child can no more be aware of its *psychic identity* than of its *physical identity*. Unable to distinguish outer from inner sensations, or sensations from feelings, it is not yet aware of a distinction between itself and its surroundings. Hence the child has no individually coherent psychic unity, or identity." (Elkin, 1958, p. 61). Irrespective of an infant's inborn traits, it is evident for Elkin that the infant's psychic identity in the primordial stage

is theorized to be *collective*. This collectivity is based on the biological necessity of "taking in" of body/milk mother and includes the unique psychical
and emotional touch of the mother, i.e., her mind-body as taste, her voice, her
handling, and feel in time-space rhythmicity. All form the basis of a unique
"sensory-I" floor. Throughout Eigen's work (*Psychotic Core*, 1986), psychic
taste buds (mouth-ego), vision (T-ego), and time-space[10] rhythmicity are sensitively and creatively explored within T-ego and body-ego language.

> The mouth is a funny kind of container, funnel, first stop toward diges-
> tion. It contains the evaluating tongue – how does it taste? Good? Bad? A
> snake in the cave of the garden of good and evil. Tongues can be wrong.
> Poisons can be doctored to taste good. One can kill oneself following
> taste. *Digestion begins with the eyes;* hands follow eyes.
>
> (Eigen, 2002, pp. 17–18; emphasis added)

This *sensory I* forms part of each individual's physical sensations as communication (hunger-pain) and instinctive feelings (bliss, joy, desire, frustration,
rage, fear) and are linked with the primordial Other. *Attraction-repulsion*
expressed in pleasure-pain is deeply embedded in the visual-skin-mouth-
mother body contact. Mother–child contact extends from the much-needed
biological to the psychological; the pleasure-pain dialectic meeting up with
the mother as psychological reality as she is repeatedly found through, and
in, the quality of her visual attention, touch, holding, tone of voice, the possible taste of milk. As mentioned, for Elkin, this forms the "primordial erotic
substratum of human life" (1958, p. 61). Given the profound interrelatedness
of self and others, the erotic substratum of human life is genuinely collective,
a collective psyche or identity (union). Eigen contributed to Elkin's work,
among many others, in recasting it in his own rich conceptual approach,
known as the *dual-union* and *distinction* structure (Eigen, 1986, 1996, 1999).
Elkin also adds that, in the primordial stage, the infant's collective-erotic
union must, in time, give way to some awareness of an individual psychic/
a personal identity *before* awareness or understanding of a body. That is,
the infant needs some mental representation of himself, a self-image *before*
he can know that "this" body belongs to "him" or "her" "self." Elkin relies
on the concepts of depersonalization and derealization as examples that an
awareness of the body-mind alone does not ensure self-awareness. An individual can certainly be aware of a/the body without being aware that it is his.
The salient question posed by Elkin in this developmental phase is, *"what
experience in the primordial stage of the child's life can give rise to the formation of an incorporeal self-image?"* (Elkin, 1958, pp. 61–62; emphasis added).
Similar to theorists such as Harry Stack Sullivan, it can be argued that the
self-image *per se* (personifications) implies an "awareness" of a distinction
between a *self*, a *non-self*, and an *Other*. Within the primordial stage, given

the infant's perceptual immaturity, the infant also cannot as yet be aware of the mother as an entity separate from the rest of his perceivable environment, although they are already in a *dual unity*. By definition, this would also include his own body, as mentioned, envisioning a sense of self earlier than the Freudian infant. *Elkin states that the infant initially experiences a primordial consciousness,* a consciousness that will forever remain mysterious as it is part of a pre-phenomenal world wherein the sense of time and space and materially (distinct subjects and objects) have not yet been subject to differentiation and maturation. This does not mean that an individual cannot access parts of this experience – or be differentiated in one area and not the other. An example may suffice. An analysand I call Pete (in Bloch & Daws, 2015, chapter 7), deeply traumatized by a psychotic mother and a genetic vulnerability to Bipolar I disorder, mentioned the following:

> Pete: I was sitting on a boat in a remote area. I looked at the moon; it came up and lit up the whole area. Suddenly from total darkness (rise of primordial consciousness). I could see all around me – it was not pitch black anymore. For a moment, I felt like *"everyman,"* which I use for the *experience I have had so many times.* It is as if all people before me and what will be after me will experience this moment the same – a *timeless moment of being.* Timeless, myself and another person long before me, we stand there at the same time; see the same thing. An *immersive brilliance of feeling;* you, me, God. All before me and after me will experience this precisely the same, unaltered. A peace gripped me. *We have immortal souls. Part of myself is time, inside a body* ... look in a mirror[11] and see a fat old man!

Similarly, Elkin writes that mystical experience and mystical participation may be ascribed to this primordial consciousness, and given man's initial lack of instinctual endowment of "early postnatal motility, *acquires mental-spiritual autonomy before acquiring physical autonomy"* (Elkin, 1972, p. 394). Pete mentioned this when he reflected on the experience of timelessness, immersive brilliance of feel, and that "w*e have immortal souls. Part of myself is time, inside a body* ... look in a mirror and see a fat old man," introducing an experiential world that predates the awareness of the natural world order (the mirror as natural world order, the body-ego), opening creative vistas in languaging those states of mind predating the natural world order. Another analysand mentioned a profoundly moving and meditative experience in visual imagery that could be interpreted as the primordial order, i.e., of *not being worded yet*:

> I went deep into meditation. An image of a very old, open book ... It had words on every page ... Deeper into the meditation ... between the pages I found myself! Between the margins, a void, where there is a white space ... Where there are no words , no story, infinity. ... A fortress[12] of

sorts. ... I contact it. ... Myself ... The search for self not defined ... Not omnipotent, not omniscient ...but spiritual ... (primordial self) ... an "*I-not-worded-yet*". ... Not storied ... Utmost openness for itself ...where we find ourselves, a *deep well* here.

I previously noted (2016) the latter as the gradual movement from a *mystical pre-Oedipal, natural order,* Oedipal, and post-Oedipal development within the dual-union distinction dialectic as described by Eigen. Each stage brings into being a unique *T-ego ∞ body-ego* participation, self–other tension, affects, representational complexity, and lived-world demands. Elkin describes the mystical pre-Oedipal as a "whole order of experience in which the subject of consciousness is not the ego, or phenomenal self" (Elkin, 1958, p. 62). That is, *mystical experiences*, as manifested in dreams, fantasies, psychotic delusions, religious ecstasy, aesthetic rapture, or erotic entrancement, "are in fact often evoked by the collective erotic unity of feeling, or *mystical participation*" (p. 62), spontaneously aroused through "physical closeness, the collective patterns of rhythm and movement, tones of voice, simple melodies of song and speech" (p. 62),[13] all primal sensations belonging to our primordial collective-erotic unity with the maternal.

It is thus essential to note the transformative link for Elkin and Eigen between the mysterious, the mystical, mystical participation and early collective-erotic co-mingling with the maternal environment as prototaxic experience. Eigen's chapter titled "Variants of mystical participation"[14] maps both the creative and destructive elements of mystical participation. Proto-qualities of being in such a state of experience remain, at times, inexpressible in general relational terms, even in adulthood, although reflecting significant psychological potential and catastrophe.

> *Total mystical experience*, at least in later life, is thus the most intense – though ineffable – of human experiences. On the one hand, it is most *dreadfull*, and may result in the shattering of the self as in *psychosis*. On the other hand, it is a most sublime experience of profound conversion, or *spiritual rebirth*. In any case, the fact that total mystical *experience involves the disruption or the regeneration of the self*, or soul, indicates that it is, essentially, a re-experience of the original process of spiritual birth and creation: *the emergence of the self and of the primordial cosmos out of the chaos of sensation-feeling*[15] *in the earliest, collective-erotic phase of infancy.*[16]
>
> (Elkin, 1958, pp. 66–67; emphasis added)

Similarly, Eigen writes:

> When I was writing *Ecstasy* (2001), I wanted to give expression to what I felt was a core experience of mine, a positive experience of life, a sense

of ecstasy in existence, a kind of credo – *the ecstasy my alcoholic patient discovered, perhaps mirroring my unconscious without knowing it, and he mirrored it for me.* A kind of *unconscious sharing*[17] without knowing we were sharing.

(2020, pp. 104–105)

From this primordial cosmos, an apprehension (psychic genesis) of an "own" psychic reality will develop in time. More specifically, through the *primordial Self's* contact and relationship with the non-self or Other, the *Self* will be transformed by both the radiant and pleasurable sensory-erotic contact as well as the very human reality of expected environmental failure. Before further development is explored, it is essential to recall that:

1. The collective unity with the mother combined with the infant's mental functioning of sensing/ ability to sense (psychic sensing equipment) serves as the foundation to the vital psycho-physiological matrix, the foundation of human psychic life.

2. Our pre-conscious collective identity (precursor to Eigen's *dual unity* concept) is not rigidly structured and serves as a background of support (or lack of it) in further development. It is similar to the *autistic-contiguous position* of Thomas Ogden, and the background of primary support as articulated by both Grotstein and Winnicott. Federn, Elkin, and Eigen also creatively rely on this developmental stage to explicate the presence of various mental-spiritual capacities as found in artists' creative "flair," understanding the domain of parapsychological sensitivity (mentalists, telepathy phenomena), the possible basis for psychosomatic catastrophes, our dream life, and our felt mysticism (Eigen, 2014a–c). Eigen returns to many of these realities in *The Psychotic Core,* the *psychotic self* as an experiential concept (1986), and his writings on spirituality (2010, 2011, 2012, 2014b, 2014c, 2018). Difficulty in this area of development naturally finds painful ruptures between *T-ego* and *body-ego* experience with its resultant impact on a sense of consciousness, the experience of time, coherence of self, and the ability to remain in contact with both self-body feeling and others. Eigen's discussion on Frank (psychosis on body-ego level) and Carl (psychosis on T-ego level) illustrates primordial terror contained in hallucinatory imagery involved primarily with either physical objects or "purely" transcendental concerns.[18]

His [Frank's] hallucinatory imagery was predominantly involved with physical objects: penis, feces, mouth, stomach, and so on … The affective atmosphere in Frank's case was heavy and thick, suffocated by feces. His fecal penis functioned almost like a fetish, something to hold on to for dear life (or death). Carl, by contrast, did not seem to know he had a penis or anus, or that feces mattered. His drama was lived out in almost purely transcendental terms. ... But the explicit terms of his hallucinations were trans-corporeal: God and the devil are pure spirits battling for his immortal soul. Eternal life or death was at stake.

(1986, pp. 95–96)

Returning to the ontogenic theory of Self, Elkin mentions the age-old view of man as a "child of God"[19] can accurately, though figuratively, be applied to the six-month-old infant's psychic state. Whatever his distinctive qualities, as determined by heredity, environmental influences, and absorption in the mother's emotional patterns, he is a fully integrated personal being who, unaware of the mother's existence, lives in total mystical communion with the primordial Other, in whose ultimately merciful love he will acquire a certain abiding sense of "basic trust." Infants who fail to achieve primordial trust may die of marasmus, although it is not difficult to think that all humans have *marasmus spots* in their psyches. Psyche growth incessantly pushes onward; that is, psychophysiological demands drive ideational and affective development forward. All are related to the survival of Selfhood. As provoked by unpleasant sensations and perceptions, fear introduces the three-month-old infant to archetypal transformations "called the primordial drama of mental-spiritual 'death and rebirth,' or regeneration" (Elkin, 1972, p. 397). The reality that the primordial Self will be exposed to the primordial Other's failings, even momentarily, "disrupts any 'Mandal experience' of an autarchic Self as identified with the Other, and the infant's internal distress transforms his sensorial perception of the primordial cosmos into a terrifying chaos" (1972, p. 397). Eigen's description of Carl, and others (Eigen, 1986, 1992, 1995), are painful reminders of such experiences of terror and chaos.

> *Carl*: I saw my own I falling apart in front of me. My ego was breaking into so many fragments. The breaking went on and on until little was left but crushed powder in blackness.

(Eigen, 1986, p. 95)

Moment-to-moment failure, developmental struggle, or a general lack of communion is registered in Elkin's and Eigen's conceptual model as being caught within "shocked-frozen-disintegration awareness," evoking, if not falling into, a *primordial anxiety* described as an "ineffable, *awe-full* or *holy* terror" (1972, p. 397), relivable in the psychosis and severe borderline states. This is also reminiscent of Winnicott's beautiful arithmetic of x+y+z wherein the Z dimension, the mother being away too long both physically and emotionally (or both), introduces intolerable anxieties, effectively interrupting the infant's *going-on-being*.

Eigen's area of faith **35**

For *whatever the actual time span* of the child's frustration, he passes through a subjective eternity of agonized *primordial doubt* about the existence of both himself and the Other. Excruciatingly aware only of his unrequited need amidst nothingness, he may then, as in the conversion of psychotic excitement into stupor, pass into a state of numb insensibility and spiritual darkness, that of *primordial despair*.

(Elkin, 1958, p. 68; emphasis added)

Transforming spiritual darkness, caught within primordial anxiety, despair, and doubt, if not psychic catatonia, can only be achieved through the merciful ministration of the Other, reminiscent of Winnicott's *Cure* (as mending the personality), and Eigen's *Rhythm of Faith*. The movement from anxiety and despair to *Cure* is akin to a *"spiritual resurrection"* (Elkin, 1958, p. 69), *awakening an even greater awareness that the self's psychic existence depends* on the merciful love of the *Other, that without trust* in the Other the primordial Self cannot remain faithful of the spiritual realm and the compassionate love evident within a primordial union. "Being-there-with" cannot be trusted, cannot even be allowed! A mental-spiritual wasteland may ensue. That is, when a child reaches out to the Other (Winnicott's x+y) due to painful hunger/need, and since there is no concept of time-space, when the other fails, the infant suffers "an eternity of dire need in the presence of a cruelly indifferent Other" (Elkin, 1966, p. 169). Furthermore, "This brings on a panic terror which, beyond a certain span, fades into an unconscious stupor that, subjectively, *is an experience of death*" (Elkin, 1966, p. 169), the eternal darkness (Eigen, 1986), Winnicott's Z dimension and 'primitive agonies," and Bion's "nameless dread." Less dramatic, although illustrative of the *"phenomenology of zero points"* (Eigen, 1986, p. 111), Eigen writes on an analysand called Lenny as follows:

What came through most of all was that Lenny, in some important sense, was not there. Flickers of life rose and fell out of and back to a baseline numbness. He had fallen out of play and out of reach, vanishing in the cherubic glow on which he floated. He had no thought about himself he wished to articulate. In his absence, psychic growth passed him by.

(1986, p. 107)

The growing awareness, as mentioned, between the mental-spiritual self and the impact of instinctual needs, leads to successive self–Other meetings consisting of pain-bliss, facilitating an experience described as the "resurrection into a blissful communion *(co-union)* with the Primordial Other," the Divine Mother–Child union (Elkin, 1966, p. 169). Successive meetings within subsequent mental-spiritual death and resurrection experiences find the child developing a growing sense of time and space, as well as trust and faith in the presence of the primordial Other to bridge intrapsychic and interpersonal realms of being – *the spiritual and natural*. Psychic atrophy and mind–body splits become ever-increasingly real for the growing child as ways to manage problematic mental-spiritual death and resurrection experiences with the primordial Other. In Eigen's striking conceptualization:

> Trouble comes and disrupts this bliss. Need, pain, distress, agony – something wrong, perhaps hunger, illness, thermal imbalance, respiratory mishap, a bad spirit. The baby lacks a material frame of reference for its distress, and the latter spirals toward infinity when the Other fails to respond and bring relief. The *radiant face-heart connection shatters* (primordial Self-Other) in the face of mounting anxiety, panic, rage (aspects of Bion's "nameless dread," Winnicott's "primitive agonies") ... From pristine radiant awakening to mental-spiritual agony and death, loss of primordial consciousness, a breaking of heart-to-heart, eye-to-eye, face-to-face contact. Simple radiant identification of primordial self with primordial Other tastes destruction.[20]
>
> (Eigen, 2004, pp. 20–21)

Clinically, Eigen's case description of *Rena* (1986, pp. 268–282) remains a detailed and felt account of loss of primordial consciousness due to annihilation horrors. If the infant is protected from eternal darkness, *resurrection* ensures a *regenerative state*,[21] and the primordial Other serves as supportive *regenerative* background. What happens if such support is absent? An analysand mentioned to me, "I cannot grow from where the destruction and collapse happened; it is no longer possible. My parents and my subsequent traumas are dead spots." Oceanic dead spots, psyche dead spots, and *T-ego* and/or *body-ego* dead spots are real.

It should also be mentioned that, even with the presence of merciful love that supports and protects,[22] the primordial Self (in primordial union) will increasingly experience (if not feel threatened by) "a *new order of values*... the *natural values*, relating to physical power and weakness, which apply to the objective, phenomenal world." (Elkin, 1958, p. 69; emphasis added). During this phase, the child becomes incrementally aware of himself not only as a primordial subject but becomes identified with his body image, allowing for a love affair with the objective world and his own body-ego capacities, à la Margaret Mahler's *practicing subphase of separation-individuation*. Being subject to natural values, experiencing omnipotence-fragility and vulnerability as a physical object in the world of larger objects give rise to a painful and frightening awareness that one may be physically injured, damaged, and annihilated. Being part of a natural order thus constitutes further fears added to the primordial Self's agonies – helpless inferiority and insignificance in terms of natural values. It is again the "merciful love and attentiveness" of the mothering Other that supports the child to take in the "mediating function" of her ministrations, enabling the painful, yet important ego expanding *negotiations between the primordial and natural world orders to proceed in service of maturation*. For Elkin the primordial contact with the numinous powerful Other serves as a basis for the "Good/Divine Mother" as well as the "Evil Mother" (predating the "bad mother") experiences. Kleinian thinking described this area of development exceptionally well, although Klein over-relies on the concept of splitting, addressed by Eigen in *Psychic Deadness* in greater detail (1996). For Elkin, it is more accurate to say the contact with the external Other is experienced in two distinct, if not archetypal, ways: Divine or Diabolic, rather than relying on splitting *per se*. In this *transitional stage* of infancy contact with the Divine Mother revives and limes feeling-memories of primal communion with the primordial, mercifully omniscient and omnipotent Other (as *Loving-Cognition*). In contrast, contact and experience with/ of the Diabolic Mother revives panic-terror (at the sight) of the wrathful, mocking, inscrutable, or cruelly indifferent Other. It is during this period that the infant is able to, with the Divine Mother, enter "upon the fully human world with joyful excitement" (Elkin, 1972, p. 402), the fully human world as bridge to the body-ego, the joy of embodiment of self-other; "passing beyond his primordial, immaterial sense of personal identity: i.e., the primordial Self now becomes an embodied entity ... The infant thus experiences himself and the mother both *with-in* and yet as palpably, concretely separate from one another – *an ambiguity that continues to mark all intimate human relations*" (Elkin, 1972, p. 402). The Divine Mother and Child relationship of the transitional stage in Western Society is best maintained through the symbolic imagery of *The Madonna and Child*. As Jungian, Elkin reminds the reader that the Divine Mother not only mediates *two world-orders* but actively protects spiritual regeneration (Eigens' death-rebirth capacity, 1986, 1996, 1998, 2020).

Concerning the Diabolical Mother, the terror at this stage is *not linked to the primordial dread of an irretrievable loss of consciousness*, or the loss of the primordial Self-Other to nothingness (Grotstein's black hole experience), but is mainly linked to phantasies of *physical destructiveness* (as described by many Kleinians), and the damaging-damaged child dramas. Eigen touches upon such realities, phenomenologically, in *The Psychotic Core* (1986), *Psychic Deadness* (1996), and *Damaged Bonds* (2001a, pp. 24–28) by describing various fright experiences seeing personality "congealed or collapsed around, or into the fright." (2001a, p. 24). The fright nucleus spreads throughout. It permeates the psyche-soma on different levels and intensities. Fright infinitizes complexes, serving as basis for the "loss of consciousness complexes" (Bion's minus links and Winnicott's Z dimensions falling into nothingness[23]), to more circumscribed areas of T-ego and body-ego corruption (disorders of self as an example). Given the developmental challenges encountered, many developmental failures are difficult to hold psychologically, contain, if ever completely "undo."[24] Although most may suffer from *temporary T-ego* and *body-ego breakdown*, those who experience "broken" dream-work will suffer immensely as the object of fright cannot be processed sufficiently (archetypal Evil Mother, Klein's bad objects). Eigen touches upon the latter in "The undreamable object" in *Damaged Bonds* (Eigen, 2001a, pp. 62–75) to be discussed shortly. Also, in Wurmser's language (in Ayers, 2003), both the *theatophilic* and the *delophilic drive* as T-ego and body-ego expressions may be injured, resulting in union terrors and paranoid adaptations, encapsulating many in the Divine-Diabolic archetypes (Eigen's psychotic self, 1986, 2016).

Furthermore, Elkin also uniquely contributed to Klein's thinking on the depressive position, moving the development from Divine–Diabolic Mother–Child drama to the more readily observable good and bad mother–child dynamics. Although a detailed comparison falls outside the scope of the current work,[25] certain developmental observations are essential to include. For Elkin, the core of the depressive position remains the infant's *growing capacity to distinguish psychical omnipotence (body-ego) from mental omniscience (T-ego)* – developmental areas Eigen addresses throughout his work in *The Electrified Tightrope* (1993, chapters 18–20) and *Psychotic Core* (1986, chapters 1–3). The infant sooner or later becomes painfully aware that both his omnipotence-omniscience and resultant holy wrath are primarily ineffective against the Diabolic Mother (indirectly ascribing omnipotence to her). The growing child also becomes increasingly aware that the Divine Mother is fallible, as she frequently gets things wrong, and may possess less direct knowledge of the child's inner life than expected (first disillusionment tempering omniscience). A more realistic image becomes increasingly *possible*. Elkin mentions that not only does the infant have greater access to his own sensations and needs in time, but "For he perceives her most *subtle expressions* of fear, anger, impatience, or disregard when *she herself is quite unaware of them*" (1972, p. 405).

Given the growing intersubjective field of knowing and relating, Elkin (1958, 1966, 1972) also included, albeit schematically, various attributes of "ideal" mothering. The various maternal features include *receptivity* (empathic responsiveness) to the child's *physical* and *mental-spiritual* gestures and feelings, providing external, if not "objective" validation to inner, subjective reality.[26] Responsiveness and receptivity support the movement from object relating to object usage in the Winnicottian sense. A lack of receptivity "encapsulates" the building blocks of play and later reverie-potentiality, and without, the psyche remains sequestered to the domain of innumerable split T-ego and body-ego adaptations. Spiritually, one may say Jericho is awaiting its Joshua.[27]

Elkin also further describes a mother able to experience and express *delight* and *joy* in both the child and *life itself*. These *affirming maternal virtues*, a *maternal aesthetic*, should be balanced by *maternal self-assurance and humility*. Lack of spontaneity and affirmation may create many developmental difficulties, mainly expressed in unlived lives, aborted self-activation, and physical-cognitive-affective-spiritual constriction. Exilic expressions of unlived lives, aborted individuation, and physical-cognitive-affective-spiritual constriction are all beautifully articulated in Eigen's *Psychic Deadness* (1996), *Damaged Bonds* (2001a), and *Toxic Nourishment* (1999). Furthermore, Eigen's trauma statements accentuate the lived reality of mutual disturbance between mother and child, dovetailing Elkin's concepts of *"mutual forgiveness"* needed for *"whole-some human love"* as seen in a *rhythm of faith* to be discussed shortly: "Through mutual forgiveness there is *spiritual love*, experienced in feelings of tenderness and esteem, or inherently, a reverence ('pity' and 'piety' in their original unity of *pietas*) that ultimately derives from the experience of communion between mother and child." (Elkin, 1966, p. 173).

When these virtues are absent, various developmental scenarios may follow and are evident in daily clinical practice (in the transference, so to speak). Where there is a lack of humility, mothering remains distant from the child's needs, in a fashion that the child is aware that the primordial Other acts as an omnipotent, omniscient Great Mother-Goddess, *unaware of maternal impact*. The child remains aware, if not totally dependent (swamped, engulfed) on her way of being; "on her ministrations and must suffer her terror-provoking stupidities, caprices, and vagaries" (Elkin, 1966, p. 173). Bollas artfully describes the latter in "Dead mother-dead child" (1999, chapter 9) and is the basis not of introjection but the "interject" (1999). For Elkin this split between the child's outer experience and his psychic situation remains the root cause of all psychopathology "insofar as it is not bridged, or reconciled, by mental-spiritual love founded on mutual forgiveness" (Elkin, 1966, p. 173), and can serve as the foundation for many contemporary difficulties in Self (disorders of Self).

If the child *fears* the mother, he may literally and figuratively close his eye and ears to her, yet still suffer dependency and mother's idiom. Again such detachment, à la Fairbairn (1984) and Guntrip (1969), brings forth many developmental tragedies and triumphs. Combined with a lack of responsiveness, the child may also be exposed to mental-spiritual disintegration, a world characterized by Dante's Inferno and Eigen's *psychotic self*; dread-full, awe-full power, homicidal destruction, and frozen fear.

If mothering lacks *humility*, although possessing the other maternal virtues, especially responsiveness to the child's feelings, the mother may become experienced as "bountiful," serving as a basis for a mutual seduction of goodness and non-communal symbiosis. The child's spontaneous physical, mental-spiritual if not emotional "self" remains developed as a "seductive mechanism,"[28] collapsing the relationship into a "mutual seduction ... a delightful game of sexual love which promotes the free development of the body-ego." (Elkin, 1966, p. 175).

With time, good enough mothering is expected to temper T-ego and body-ego intensities, supporting psyche-soma differentiation and integration. With integration, the body-ego is expected to become the seat of Freud's Eros and Thanatos and the T-ego the seat of Logos. Both ego structures start from *impersonal worlding*, and adequate holding by parents find a greater humanizing of the world and Other, as well as the body and the T-ego. Thoughts-feelings become part of a growing personal-communal as opposed to the manic-symbiotic[29] relations characterized by manipulative/psychopathic embodied ego structures, detachment through schizoid withdrawal, or being collectivized, in essence losing one's subjectivity – being wiped out and wiping out. Again, infinite variations are possible. As an example, when the T-ego, even if orientated to reality, short-circuits body-ego adaptations and denies the importance of libidinal vicissitudes of the body-ego, one may find a cold, detached schizoid-like T-ego described by Eigen as the *mind object* (Eigen, in Corrigan & Gordon, 1995). For Eigen, the *T-ego ↔ body-ego split* is of utmost importance in modern psychoanalysis with both growth and pathology implications:

> In my books and papers, *I explore aspects of a split between occultly transcendent mental self and fusional-explosive body self. This split is the core psychopathological structure of our time.* ... Ideal feeling may take the form of omniscience in mental self, omnipotence in the body self. Omniscience-omnipotence often fills gaps where one might sense deficit ... The complexity of relationships between terms of experience may prompt us to side with one term against the other (splitting), rather than to stay alive to the play of *similarity-difference.* We are engaged in a long-term learning process, thousands of years old, in which we dimly apprehend workings of the diverse capacities that make us up and carry us along. *Our destiny is to become partners with our capacities.*
>
> (1996, pp. 103–104; emphasis added)

Eigen's synoptic discussion also succinctly summarizes Elkin's thinking on the three main structural forms of embodied Selfhood[30] reflected in developmental difficulty. They are the communal, the psychopathic and the collectivized ego segments that reflect the original divisions of our T-ego and body-ego. Elkin mentions that "the schizoid ego, the seat of mental-spiritual alienation, and the id, the seat of repressed libidinal and aggressive impulses, give rise to psychic illness in the nonpsychotic human being" (1972, p. 414). All psychotherapy aims to reintegrate as far as possible these two split-off entities and aims at the "(1) ... elimination of the superego and of its conjoined collectivized ego, schizoid ego, and id, and (2) the creative structuring of Selfhood by the progressive dissolution of the autistic-psychopathic ego, into an all-inclusive personal-communal ego" (1972, p. 414). For me, Elkin's description dovetails

Eigen's distinction-union dialectic in a rhythm of faith psychology beautifully. Finally, for Elkin:

> The resulting despair of the total ego, or Self, is then perpetuated in the schizoid quality, or split, between the T-ego and the body-ego. In our twentieth century, this crucial break in human experience has been recognized, as the "depressive position," to be the ultimate root of all psychic illness. From ancient times it has remained in mythical consciousness as the theme of the Lost Paradise. *At any rate, this psychic split, experienced as a broken heart, is the universal and forever underlying experience of tragedy in human life.* Thus it must somehow be treated, explicitly or not, by all methods of psychic healing. In modern psychotherapy, a radical cure, by re-experiencing the *original harmony between the T-ego and the body-ego*, requires a *psychic regression to communion with the Good Mother*, now in the image of the therapist. The healing or "salvation" that most nearly approximates this in the religious tradition is doubtless the identification with Christ, an image of the incarnated Primordial Self, in *symbolic crucifixion and resurrection. In the one instance, the therapeutic goal is "basic trust"; in the other, "faith in (the living) God."*
>
> (Elkin, 1972, pp. 171–172; emphasis added)

Winnicott's ontology of transitional relatedness, our primal agonies, and hope

Before formally meeting Winnicott in 1968, Eigen mentions that he initially "found" Winnicott in Elkin's office somewhat "randomly," leafing through Elkin's many books (Eigen, 2016). From Eigen's early writing on transitional space, object usage, and object relating[31] in *The Electrified Tightrope* (1993, chapter 4) and *Expressive Therapy* (Robbins, 1986) to Eigen's volumes such as *Toxic Nourishment* (1999), *Emotional Storm* (2005), *Contact with the Depths* (2011), and *Faith* (2014b, chapters 3 and 4), we meet a Winnicott that accentuates vital moment-to-moment affective shifts in the mother–infant dyad, a formative infant in need of being-*Being*, to a Winnicott that describes the native self as able to spontaneously grow and recover from the *creation and destruction of its objects*.[32] The innate maturational tendency, the archetypal soul need to become an *integrated-whole-ongoing-being* within a facilitating environment, implies the successful *use* of *absolute dependence, creative destruction,* and *psychic holding*. Psychic holding suggests an ability to hold the infant (maternal percipience, sagacity, receptiveness, humility) in the intermediate area within a given time and space. An intimate process of mother–child adapting and growing alongside each other to minimize the inherent moments of lack and failure. This is similar to Elkin's pristine awakening, as failure could culminate in immutable experiences of impingement and disinte-gration, frequently transforming into a *fear of breakdown* (Khan, 1963, 1972). The fear of breakdown for both Winnicott and Eigen serves as a psychic signal of *breakdown already experienced* and calls for myriad *defensive forms of pro-tection* against unthinkable anxieties. From his work on clinical regression, 1955 to 1971, Winnicott's "Fear of Breakdown" (1974) paper summarizes the various primitive anxieties and their respective defenses as follows:

a)   A return to an unintegrated state, the defense being disintegration.
b)   Falling forever, the defense being self-holding.
c)   The loss of psych-somatic integration and its resulting failure of indwelling, the defense being depersonalization.
d)   A loss of sense of what is real, the defense being the misuse of primary narcissism, and finally,
e)   The loss of the capacity to relate with, and to, objects. The defenses being mainly autistic in nature, exclusionary, primarily relating to self-phenomena, etc.

Winnicott would also mention that, even in psychotic illness, it may serve us better to think of it not as a breakdown but rather as a defensive organiza-tion in relation to a primal agony. This reality can clearly be read in Eigen's *Psychotic Core* (1986) case studies. In essence, as Eigen is very aware of the psychic existence of primitive agonies, Eigen's Winnicott is deeply involved in articulating what it means to be free, to feel alive, be oneself, be "abled," and "allowed" to both "create"[33] and survive. In true Eigenesque fashion, this would imply "shedding language skins" (1993, p. 70) *in search of an area of freedom*, free from even psychoanalysis's obsessive symbol hunting tendencies. As will soon be evident, and similar to Elkin's conceptualizations discussed, *coming through* the facticity of our *dual-union with the Other* (in developing two distinct subjectivities in object usage), our maturational capacity and need for distinction, finding distinction-in-union and union-in-distinction[34] "in order to link up with the experiencing that is fed by, yet transcends, dualistic categories" (1991, p. 71), all serve as a basis for Eigen's *Rhythm of Faith* and reading of Winnicott. To return to Eigen's chapter titled "The area of faith in Winnicott, Lacan, and Bion" (1993, chapter 11), Eigen provides the reader with a provisional Winnicottian informed developmental thesis, stating:

> In transitional experiencing the infant *lives through a faith that is prior to a clear realization of self and other differences*; in object usage the infant's faith takes this *difference into account*, in some sense is based on it. In contrast, the introjective-projective aspect of the self is involved in splitting and hiding processes, and inherently self-bound psychic web-spinning in which the possibility of faith is foreclosed [in object

relating] … My immediate concern is the way object–usage takes the life of faith in transitional experience forward, and the role of introjective-projective processes plays as a foil to its unfolding. My aim is to show how faith evolves from transitional experiencing through object usage, in part by transcending (or undercutting) introjective-projective ordeals and barriers.

(1993, p. 110; emphasis added)

Synoptically, and similar to Elkin's primordial consciousness (embedded in a collective), Eigen traces the developmental stages of Winnicott's maturational approach to a *primordial faith*, that is, a faith that the infant lives through *before* the realization of self–other differentiation may be evident in object usage. For Winnicott, transitional experience may be situated between the emergence of infantile consciousness and the infant's growing awareness of the mothering other. This period of "self," can be somewhat summarized by the song by Crosby, Stills, Nash, and Young titled *Helplessly Hoping* (1969), wherein one finds beautiful descriptions of the need for another to fill the internal world, awaiting the Other, poignantly:

They are *one person*
They are *two alone*
They are *three together*
They are for each other

The *transitional area self* is neither singular nor differentiated, but rather *for* each other. More specifically, in the *transitional area self*, the experience of self as the creator is taken for granted, unimpinged, and "pre" the "intimate environment." As the core self is born, so is the Other (baby and mother are born, birthed as a psyche unit). In the transitional area, the primordial self (Elkin's *T-ego*) remains for itself the ultimate creator/creation, immersed in rapture. In time, a *unit self* is bound to develop, characterized by self-delimitation, body-ego impingements, and the growing importance of the Other, very similar to Elkin's post-four-months infant. If all goes well, the transitional area can hold, so to speak, impingements and optimal levels of frustration. It is expected that such holding would both allow and support the growing infant to *retain his creative abilities and ability to create.* Paradoxically, such creativity and inner life remain reliant on, and in need of, an experience of omnipotence, omniscience, and illusion. Gradually, inner creativity will increasingly come into contact with the Other, external reality, the "not-me," introducing the notion of the subjective and objective self-(M)other. The transitional area makes use of the transitional object (s), enabling an infant/child to remain with itself as it bridges to the "not-me." Both phantasy and facticity (mental-spiritual and natural world order values) come into an ever-growing relationship, able to enrich each other without traumatic rupture, false self adaptations, primal agonies, or normotic adjustments.

Eigen mentions that the latter may be subject to foreclose given the *psychic-webspinning dilemmas* evident in the stage of *object-relating* (although the faith of the Other remains of utmost importance here, too!). Being able to transition from the *area of object relating* to the growing possibility and *area of concern through object usage and transitional experiencing*[35] sees "faith" taking on a new dimension. That is, both the self and the Object survive instinctual true self-articulation, ruthless as it may be, without collapse into reactionary adaptations from the Other (impingements). More specifically, the infant's innocent ruthlessness is met with holding, not retaliation or impingements that would lead to the cultivation of hate. Impingements and reactionary attacks necessitate pathological accommodations (Brandchaft, Doctors, & Sorter, 2010). Such adaptations come close to Elkin's maternal values of lack and fear of the mother, and Eigen's work on the psychotic self (1986), deadened self (1996), *Toxic Nourishment* (1999), and *Damaged Bonds* (2001a). Psychological birth relies on creativity, the inherent uncompromised faith to find and destroy objects and symbols in the transitional area. Winnicott's *creating-in-relating* and *relating-in-creating dialectic*[36] transcend the *"control or reparation"* orientated psychologies (more in the area of object relating), as important as it is. In Eigen's reading, Winnicott's genius is based on his descriptive psychology of how so-called destructiveness, one's true self-creative (innocent ruthlessness) intensity, can be lovingly met by the Other in the area of the object subjectively created, the subjective object, and survive, so that the object can be objectively created in time, and that the objective object may come into being as a source of *further joyful contact and creation*. Think here of Green's and Bion's connection and holding of Eigen's creative intensities: "You stole my work" (to Green), "you are joyless" (Bion). With the (M)other's birth as an actual separate Other in relation to an individual self, true joy may become possible. Both Winnicott and Eigen balance contemporary control-mastery-reparation models (Freudian and Kleinian) with *a joy-based model, orphic in essence,*

> He [Winnicott] seeks a moment in which destruction plays a creative role in constituting a world outside me, one that can be used for my development because it can survive or "take" my development. I have called this a *joy-based model*, but it is more than joy, although delight, surprise, amazement may be part of *awakening to the realness of reality, an emergent sense of the real: reality can be all this!* Perhaps one can say there is a *sense of the realness of realness. It is a moment in which destructiveness does not have to be controlled or atoned for, but can breathe, enter into feeling communion, and further creation/discovery*[37] *of feeling.*
>
> (2014, p. 26; emphasis added)

Of course, much can go wrong, much does go wrong, and Winnicott and Eigen are not naïve analysts. However, psychoanalytic faith in transitional space allows each to remain available in their unique ways. Eigen also adds that Winnicott's transitional experiencing and phenomena are not to be confused with the use of transitional objects as primarily tranquilizers or objects that are held onto as *tranquilizers* as they "mark a rupture between the infant and the realm of creative experiencing, which it may seek *to close by self-soothing*" (Eigen, 1993, p. 111). An analysand reflected: "After my husband died, I started to buy animal stuffies compulsively. I stuff them everywhere! Hundreds, I can't stop buying them!"

To return to Winnicott, Eigen accentuates the reality that the transitional dimension primarily sees a heightened, open, and fluid experience of creativity.[38] Within the transitional area, the self and the other are neither singular nor a twoness *per se*, but make up the first not-me-not-wholly-the-other-but-something-more. The Other is also in becoming; as mentioned previously, Otherness is birthed (the Real). A continual Self–Other birthing and interpenetrating creativity within the background of dual-union and distinction-union is possible, similar to the first few months of Elkin's model and Balint's interpenetrating harmonious mix-up conceptualization. This creative potential is taken for granted as well as the fit with the Other (and thus "world" in general). The self–other birthing is in itself the fundamental process of creativity,

> For Winnicott, in contrast to Freud and Klein, creativity permeates psychic life and is involved in the very birth of self and other, a process more fundamental than *substitutive strivings*. Creativity is itself a primary term of human experience. For Winnicott, the *defensive use of creativity is a secondary development and not the home ground of the human self.*
>
> (1993, p. 111; emphasis added)

For Eigen, in contrast with transitional experience (Elkin's originary spiritual I-Thou?) and the possibility of *object usage, object relating* remains bound by projective-introjective operations of a/the unit self. The Other is undoubtedly meaningful but remains in the orbit of the unit self's omnipotence-omniscience warps. Eigen repeatedly returns to this theme and its impact in corrupting the mind-ego and body-ego.[39] By definition, in object relating, the mother–child orbit is meaningful as to structuralize the self (fueled by "autarchic introjective-projective operations"). However, primordial faith in union, rapt immersion, transitional experiences, and capacity for concern remain rather limited as the self fails to bridge to the Other as found in *object usage*. A closed intrapsychic system is exposed to both the Divine and Diabolical, the inner world populated by devils and ghosts. It is hoped that in object relating, the autarchic introjective-projective operations (Eigen, 1993, p. 112) will be "re"-exposed to a new *awakening* in *object usage*. In more creative and poetic developmental language, the closed omnipotent self-other experience is *reborn* into a new awareness that the Other is "wholly other" (1993, p. 112), outside the unit self's control. As such, the *unit self* of object relating is informed of *a new possible psychic and experiential triptych, i.e., the experience of isolation, true relatedness, and transcendence.* All are signposts and can be returned to in creative and non-creative ways. The "outside one's boundaries" can be both frightening and disorganizing, although enlivening. New freedom and aliveness in self and in relation to the Other become increasingly possible. *The second birth,*[40] in my "Eigen" understanding, finds the primordial substrate of the psyche exposed in time, within sensitive dosing, to the reality of continual developmental mourning (Eigen's death–resurrection rhythms of both Self and Other) in the transitional area, evoking creative protest. The very life-giving separation processes, the psyche's painful rebirthing supports the ever-growing capacity for awareness of "in" –"side" and "out"-"side." The protest, if not at times anger, or Winnicott's destructive attacks on the object, serve as a foundation to the experience of *faith in externality:*

> What is emerging is the sense of externality as imperishable living fact and principle. ... *It is this intersection of profound vulnerability [of self and attacked Other] and saving indestructibility that brings the paradox of faith to a new level.*
>
> (Eigen, 1993, p. 113; emphasis added)

Eigen accentuates Winnicott's notion that this destruction, part of differentiation and further articulation of self in faith, continues in unconscious phantasy. A rich psychoanalytic contribution, that is, a creative unconscious background of phantasy of destruction–rebirth with self–Other *able to withstand such growth, of a continuously coming-through.* For Eigen, this is the *joyous experience of difference as coming through, feeling real to each other.* It also implies moving well beyond Freudian (control), and Kleinian (reparation) guilt epistemologies, as the infant is allowed to give its instinctual self (I AM) full reign, followed by the Other remaining welcoming in holding and supporting the infant to experience the complex affective experiences evident in true self-activation. This may, by definition, include the experience of guilt and other qualities of concern. Eigen's capacity for concern implies joy in the integrity of coming through together and is in no need for reparation *per se*, although it would not exclude it! It is of interest to note that for Eigen, Kleinian reparation is in itself a subtle form of megalomania, that is, the fear and need to repair imagined damage may in essence still reflect being subject to psychic web-spinning; "There can be no true otherness where the infant is concerned for mother because of a phantasy of destructiveness he tries to undo ... This *I love you* does not make up for *I destroy you, but turns the latter to good use.*" (1993, pp. 116–117; emphasis added). From this logic, the well-known psychoanalytic dictum:

> *The subject says to the object*: "I destroyed you," and the object is there to receive the communication. From now on the subject says: "Hullo object!" "I destroyed you." "I love you." "You have value for me because of your survival of my destruction of you." "While I am loving you I am all the time destroying you in (unconscious) phantasy."[41]
>
> (Eigen, 1993, pp. 116–117)

Winnicott's unique psychosomatic self-in-transition dialectic further reflects on the notion that no individual escapes the complexity of their own sensitivity and I AM. So too, the various adjustments to be made given impacts (impingements) to the nascent self as the self comes into *Being*, a process frequently overstraining the infant, foreclosing the use of transitional experience with various consequences. Despite being subject to the vagarities of impingement, retreat into isolation may still hold the seeds of rebirth. The latter forms a central part of Eigen's beautifully written 1973 article, "Abstinence and the schizoid ego." Eigen's unique interpretation of regression as creative isolation for rebirth can be read in tandem with the great Carl Jung's approach to regeneration, our inherent *Harpocrates need, if not orphic spark*.[42] Before the god of silence, healing needs to "hold" its energy to allow and hear the autochthonous I's inner voice for transformation. The movement from transitional experiencing to object-relating and object-usage finds in many of Eigen's works that Faith in the Other remains imperative as all development must face *deprivation ↔ privation* trauma within wounded nourishment realities. Madness, far from the exclusionary domain of psychiatric nomenclature, evident in everyday agonies, finds analysands struggling to experience somato-psychic integration, warding off fears of loss of self, loss of mind, loss of good self feel, loss of psychosomatic unity, and feeling trapped in an endless and painful return of the same. In Eigen's Winnicott, "For the madness Winnicott speaks of has as its nucleus not only fear of physical death, but also psychological agonies over loss of mind and self and functioning, inchoate dreads involving unbearable impacts as self comes into being" (2004, p. 22). Overstrain, deformation of self (see Eigen, 2004, p. 22), and disintegration all form a complex dialectic in both Winnicottian and Eigenesque thinking.[43] Given Eigen's writing on temporality, primary process failures, damaged bonds-damaged dreamwork, the psychotic core, psychic deadness, variations of personal aloneness,[44] and the trauma-nourishment impact of mother's presence-absence,[45] it may be of importance to synoptically review Winnicott's transformative developmental equation as found in *Playing and Reality*, notably chapter 7, titled, the "Location of Cultural Experience." That is, returning to the concept of the infant's development progression towards object-usage and Winnicott's location chapter, Winnicott states that the feeling of the primary Other's existence lasts x minutes and that the imago of the Other will fade if the Other is away more than x minutes. With the fading of the imago so does the infant's capacity to make optimal psychological use of the symbol of the union.[46] Distress follows, and it is hoped that the mother returns in time, in x+ y minutes (on time, see Eigen and Govrin, 2007). Although distress has been evident, the x+y rhythm does not *alter* the infant as the mother mends[47] the infant's state. Yet, trauma may ensue if the mother does not return in time to support the infant in his distress. Trauma and madness for Winnicott are linked to *a break in life's continuity*, necessitating primitive defenses to become organized as to defend against a repetition of "unthinkable anxiety" or the return of a confused state. Given the breakup the baby has to

> *start again permanently deprived* of the *root* which could provide *continuity with personal beginning* ... By contrast, from the effects of x+ y+z degree of deprivation, babies are constantly *cured* by the mother's localized spoiling that *mends* the ego structure. This mending of the ego structure re-establishes the baby's capacity to *use a symbol of union*; the baby then comes once more to allow and even to *benefit from separation. This is the place that I have set out to examine, the separation that is not a separation but a form of union.*
>
> (Winnicott, 1971, pp. 97–98: emphasis added)

An analysand stated Winnicott's description as follows, "Nobody truly provided for me. It's a horrid shameful mess to be endured. Ripped off, scammed. There is no relief-package to restore me. I feel ushered into damage, left with damage ... I just have damage to show. My whole life a stop-start-stop-start experience..." For both Eigen and Winnicott, such trauma necessitates various False Self adaptations, adaptations unable to make use of transitional relatedness in creative and curative ways. That is, as the generative distinction–union rhythm is foreclosed, the infant remains caught in omnipotence, omniscience, and premature psychic foreclosure, themes of great importance to Eigen. Finally, given the reality of trauma and false self-adaptation, Eigen sensitively remarks, "The false self is a privileged system of counterparts or substitutes. It does not realize that victory weakens it. By absorbing the true self, it cuts itself off from the larger destiny of existence" (1996, pp. 105–106).

Bion's ontology of O, the murderous superego, and the importance of psychoanalytic faith

As with the work of Winnicott, the writings of Wilfred Bion remain breathtaking in scope, conceptual depth, and emotional rawness. As a psychoanalyst, soul ontologist, and epistemologist, I hold Bion the Plato of psychoanalysis.

For Eigen, Bion's work can be conceptualized as a profoundly meditative stance on the "psyche's inability to tolerate experiencing" (1998, p. 97). The various psychological modes or attitudes operative in such inability may include mind-lessness and hallucination (see especially Eigen, 1986, pp. 114–138), surviving superego malevolence (Eigen, 1996, 1998, 1999, 2001a), laboring under psychic equipment deficits (Eigen, 1996, 2001a), and the importance of knowing and nurturing our embryonic self (Eigen, 2016, 2018, 2021). Specifically, and with greater application value than the day-to-day psychoanalytic use of *deficiency*, our embryonic nature introduces an area of *too much ↔ too little,* bringing into focus the dialect between our *perennial embryonic ↔ malevolent self and other* as well as Faith in Ultimate Reality, or F in O (faith in the area of catastrophe and hope). According to Eigen's Bion, the human race to date has primarily focused on psyche growth reliant on control-mastering adaptations exclusively. It may not have as yet developed the capacity to tolerate emotional truth needed for psyche-integrity; "Bion notes that the human race is ill-equipped to tolerate its own experiential capacity. It naturally orients itself toward external objects and the task of survival" (Eigen, 1986, p. 138). Bion and Eigen are not referring to a moral position, not the still small voice found in superego-based adaptations, but rather, a deeply held conviction that new ways of being a person, a person in becoming, remains a frightening prospect – *the nasty business of being and becoming oneself.* Experience, its impact, and implications cannot be fully assimilated or accommodated by a single psyche, even more so, in the very working with the experience experienced we may be exposed to, or produce states our psyche and its equipment cannot sufficiently handle. "We are too much (or too little) for ourselves." (Eigen, 1998, p. 100). We evacuate and turn off our capacities, our exquisite sensitivities, our inherent autochtonous ways of *getting at and into experience needed for a truthful experience.* Bion and Eigen state that if we could accept our embryonic nature, our deficits, even make room for it, we may become aware of what we can and cannot do, that is, not overburden, strain, or overload our capacities. Even more so, "We may try to do too much, overextend ourselves (think Winnicott's' overstrain!), substitute omnipotence for openness, *ravage ourselves with mastery rather than discover what partnership can mean*" (1998, p. 100).

Given Bion's painful childhood, an immense succession of personal losses, soul loneliness, wartime trauma, and psychiatric practice specializing in the psychosis, it is not strange to read that Bion's infant remains somewhat different from the Fairbarnian or Winnicottian infant, as it is expected from psychological birth to survive the most malevolent of psychic forces, forces communicating – *thou shalt not be alive*[48] *(the murderous superego).* The concept of malevolence in Bion's work is frequently characterized as a hypertrophied superego, hidden, at times, in plain sight, that is, secondary process thinking,[49] functioning as a life-condemning tendency – *an id and ego destroying superego.* Malevolence may even damage the very psychic processor needed to metabolize trauma (see the chapter on psychic deadness), undoing not only psychic work but the mental capacities needed for such work (attacks on linking and attacks on the mental apparatus). Empirical psychoanalytic studies have frequently found that, for example, delusional disorders show difficulty in various areas of logic and knowing (-K), schizophrenic patients often struggle within *hyper-reflexivity,*[50] and psychosomatic patients project-ively identify their bodies (T-ego shrapnel lodged in body-ego). Damaged psyche processors, damaged primary and secondary process thinking (Bion's lack of no-thing, rigid causal thinking) forecloses the full range of affective experiencing, the successful breakthrough and breakdown in metabolizing and reworking traumatic impacts that, in turn, warp sensing (*Beta elements*)-feeling-thinking-dreaming capacity, if not the very space it inhabits (or inhabited) endopsychically and then interpersonally. Various examples are evident throughout Eigen's work, most notably the *Psychotic Core* (1986), *Psychic Deadness* (1996), the case study volumes (1992, 1995), *Toxic Nourishment* (1999), *Damaged Bonds* (2001a), *Emotional Storm* (2005), and *Feeling Matters* (2007) that I will return to in upcoming chapters. Temporality, spatiality, and stretching along (being) may be ripped and torn, replaced with intolerance, explosiveness, agitation, collapse, unsatisfying hollowing-out, and entropy (gravity) type demands.

> A crippled primary process can not begin the transmutation of raw trauma globs into useable feeling/imagining/thinking flows. Raw, unprocessed-unprocessable trauma globs, together with chards of aborted, deformed thoughts-affects (scraps of failed psychic movement), agglutinate and fur-ther block possibility for movement. One may depict this state as stagnant, a graveyard, or garbage heap: a dead or inert or wasted psyche ... The psyche is at once dead and radioactive: its deadness takes on a poisonous life of its own, contaminating and destroying whatever comes near.
>
> (Eigen, 1998, p. 98)

Bion's theory of thinking, his *psyche starting point,* is based on transforming so-called *beta-elements* (*β elements,* unmetabolized sensory-affective experi-ence) into *alpha-elements* (*α elements* as thoughts that the thinker can think), nourishing the psyche. Through contact with maternal *reverie,* the caretaking role provides an αfunction, transforming unmetabolized sensory-affective experience into "thoughts" that can be "thought" by the *thinker-coming-into-being Being.* Within such an imagined psychological big bang, the necessary metabolizing mental process, *β elements* as undigested facts are transformed by alpha-function into alpha-elements that can be repressed, become stor-able, and available for dream thoughts. Beta-elements cannot be repressed or used for learning *per se* and can only be *used* for projective identification and acting out. Hope and faith still exist in projection, projective identification, and acting out, reflecting the very catastrophe(s) the psyche has initially been exposed to. If alpha-functioning fails endopsychically and interpersonally, that is, the container remains unable to support transformations needed for dreaming, the construction of visual images, learning, affective thinking, and symbolization remain vulnerable. In Eigen's evocative language, "For Bion, the catastrophic nature of its own life is the first and most basic task the psyche must take up" (1986, p. 134). As mentioned, this is achieved by the growth of the signal capacity to communicate such an inner world to another.

> It is the psyche's basic job to transmute initial catastrophic globs of experience into *psychically soluble events*. Bion calls the capacity to do this alpha function. The great creation-destruction myths, so basic a part of religious and psychotic imagery, express this transformational work ... Beta elements are gestated by alpha function into an alive affective thinking process.
>
> (Eigen, 1986, p. 134)

Also,

> A concern in Bion's work is *ability* or failed *ability to process catastrophic impacts. We nibble, choke, chew on bits of catastrophe, traumatized affect globs that freeze, paralyze, galvanize us* ... Except it is unclear what nutrient catastrophic affects contain – perhaps simply ability to feel and the quality of that ability. *Trauma destroys and nourishes* ...
>
> (Eigen, 2007, p. 51; emphasis added)

The alive and enlivening affective thinking process includes dream-work, *archetypal or mystic systems* so beautifully described by Eigen (see 1986, pp. 52–65), C. G. Jung, and Erich Neumann; signs to symbols, reflective functioning, and finally, the capacity for a theory of mind, and more! Eigen mentions that, for the psychotic self or core, one could hold: "The psychotic patient signals rather than symbolizes his ongoing sense of catastrophe. The material he uses may resemble symbols, but they are used to point to an unnameable psychic reality. Similarly, the borderline patient must often be taught to link up words and feelings" (1986, p. 133). Even more concerning, and to be addressed in later chapters in this volume, in the psychotic process, "the transmuting of beta elements into food for thought runs amok, the process may even be thrown into reverse gear. The personality may collapse to a point at which raw beta elements run wild." (1986, p. 34). Unborn thoughts, still-born thoughts, corrupted mind-body thoughts and feelings may ensue, creating a kind of *toxic mental-metabolic condition* (see Eigen, 1986, pp. 314–322). We *are* and *become* resistance, resistance to the self, and the Real. Eigen writes, "On a personality level, we should coin the term, *self-resistance*." (Eigen, 2016, p. 8).

Given the impact of the Real and the presence of our catastrophic nature, there is much to resist. However, both Eigen and Bion move toward the catastrophe with much openness (see F in O), "*For Bion, the self is born, evolves, and dies with a sense of catastrophe*" (1986, p. 135: emphasis added). How can growth be promoted, the ongoing sense of being supported, if the self is so inclined? For both Bion and Eigen, *a way* of working with our human catastrophe is by adopting and cultivating a somewhat radical notion, that of faith (F). Similar to the misuse of the transitional object as a narcotizing fetish rather than a transformational symbol, faith, as held by Bion and Eigen, is not used as a "self-soothing opiate" (1986, p. 135), but rather, a way of experiencing experience openheartedly through creative surrendering, welcoming the most obstructive and obdurate states of mind just as one wants to control, recoil, or master; "By the area of faith I mean to point to a way of experiencing that is undertaken with one's whole being, all-out, 'with all one's heart, with all one's soul, and with all one's might'" (1993, p. 109). For Bion, a radical openness is needed to meet experience wholeheartedly so as to develop our embryonic capacities. Such meeting should be attempted without memory, understanding, and desire. Abstaining remains problematic as our development and cultural expectations are primarily based on control-mastery vectors. Suspending thinking-feeling-control-mastery attachments in faith to the emotional reality of the moment (Bion's O, or ultimate unknowable reality) remains an evolutionary task for both Eigen and Bion. Eigen writes:

> Thus, F in O approaches an attitude of pure receptiveness. It is an alert readiness, an alive waiting[51] ... Bion describes how uncomfortable one may be in this open state. One must tolerate fragmentation, whirls of bits and pieces of meaning and meaninglessness, chaotic blankness, dry periods, and psychic dust storms.
>
> (1986, p. 136)

> In a sense, faith fights catastrophe with catastrophe. It can shatter our attempt to cling to well-intentioned security systems. Contact with a catastrophic reality shatters the lies we have built up to protect ourselves ... Faith thrives at our cutting edge. It sustains our approach to and our tolerance of ourselves. It keeps our sensitivity to ourselves alive. Our personality deepens when we are led by F in O.
>
> (1986, p. 138)

> F in O opens up to the pristine catastrophe of psychic birth.
>
> (1986, p. 137)

Holding "with"-"in" damaged bonds, catastrophic impacts, poisonous residue, and various other "irritants," as well as living through an experience rather than being destroyed or further ruptured by it, remains a deep orphic wish in both Eigen's and Bion's work. Eigen frequently writes how we as analysts attempt to rid ourselves of ourselves, our patients, parts of our patients, hoping to make life and the encounter more "peaceful," but it remains a problem only postponed. Patients and the difficulties faced may be too much, necessitating foreclosure. For Eigen, there is a price to pay for both avoiding and working with trauma–nourishment, if not our most wounded selves. Tolerating our destructive natures and processes remains a creative activity, a human feat in and of itself. As previously written (Daws, in Bloch & Daws, 2015, p. 114), Eigen's work *per se* serves as a welcoming other (alpha-functioning), a psychoanalytic vision that serves the needed auxiliary support to process affect globs, enabling emotional digestion even when it entails remaining in contact with the colicky parts of life, having to manage emotional shingles, or meeting a self that is enslaved and entombed. As will be evident in Part II of this volume, coming alive (Eigen, 1986, 1999, 2001a) carries its own risks; that is, *aliveness carries the burden of possible re-traumatization.* Despite the various known and unknown dangers of being oneself, "all growth, limited though it may be, is expected to bring forth the very capacity to not only re-experience wounded-nourishment and its vicissitudes, that is, the various endopsychic, interpersonal, and communal/cultural forces of self-estrangement, but also a *renewed hope* that the native self may germinate" (Daws, in Bloch & Daws, 2015, p. 114). Such renewed hope, faith, F in O, can be found in Eigen's use of Bion's notion of alpha-function as laboring disability, and the close conjunction between self-creation, Federn's I "feeling," and the moment of destruction in meeting up with the wounding–obstructive–obdurate object.

> Alpha function, then, labors with a chronic disability, *injured by the injury* it works with. Yet it is driven to process damaging forces as part of the way it heals itself, risking further injury by seeking health … To assemble anything means to assemble what destroys one … To constitute a living person within oneself is to constitute what is destroying this person as well. The analyst must dream what destroys the patient's dreams, and since the analyst may or may not be much better at this than the patient, the analyst turns on two people becoming partners in evolution, doing work all humanity must come to do. *In other words, part of the long-term work involves becoming real to ourselves and each other and the profound ethic this implies.*
>
> (Eigen, 2004, p. 32; emphasis added)

Furthermore, according to Eigen, Bion's O[52] represents the psyche's capacity and need for a "profound-dialogue-with" emotional truth (1986, p. 133). Such a dialogue, not allocated to a specific *psychological locus per se*, imagines the analysand able to experience *experience* in an open, undefensive, even transcendental way:

What evolves in analysis is no mere knowledge about content, or pleasurable ways of interaction, or more successful adaptations. These may be involved but are not primary. *The most precious gain is the evolution of openness towards experiencing*, or, as Bion writes, "experiencing experience," a process in which something more is always happening (or about to)[horizon of possibility]. *The essential freedom analysis brings is the analytic attitude itself, the liberation of the capacity to focus on O.*

(1993, p. 133: emphasiscs added)

Cultivating an *in-"tune"-ment* with the movement of O, according to Eigen, implies a measure of independence from our inherent pleasure–pain and control–mastery dialectic. Such independence supports moments of open attentiveness wherein the emotional truth of self and one's lived world becomes a transformational possibility. Knowing oneself or the emotional truth about a situation also brings into sharp focus the very forces that will work against such knowledge. Surviving such opening–closing psychological processes in search of O may be possible given the cultivation of a *"Rhythm of Faith."*

Eigen's transformative rhythm of faith

As mentioned in the introduction, Eigen's concept of "rhythm of faith" (2004, p. 33) introduces the reader to Elkin's psychoanalytic and developmental vision as well as combining his notions on the *merciful love of the Other* with Donald Winnicott's *spontaneous recovery* and Wilfred Bion's *coming alive.* That is, for Eigen, the "rhythm of faith" includes Elkin's notion of death and rebirth, Winnicott's notions of breakdown and recovery, as well as Bion's sense of being murdered as one comes alive. Eigen's "rhythm of faith" maps the infinite variations and permutations of our psyche's growth–collapse, nurture–trauma, and the "trauma globs" in need of "transmutations" into "useable feeling/imagining/thinking flows" (1995, p. 113). For Eigen, "trauma globs" are inevitable given our lopsidedness, the facticity of our perennial obstructive–wounding–obdurate Self/Other spirals, in need of deep "Faith," even within analysis itself.

In analysis the patient experiences the analyst variously as a traumatic force or wounding object, supportive background presence, vehicle of wisdom and stupidity, auxiliary dream-worker, agent of faith. The experiential arc described here constitutes a rhythm of faith. *For Elkin faith evolves and is sustained as the primordial self is nursed through despair and stupor, quickening into life with the Other's help.*

(Eigen, 2004, p. 34; emphasis added)

That is, faith, as held by Elkin, is the consequence of good enough midwifery expected to *initiate* and *sustain a mental-spiritual breakdown–recovery rhythm* (as found in Eigen, 1973). Within Elkin's developmental rhythm, "Faith" is born, if not reborn, in the Other's capacity to serve as a midwife wherein sustainment is expected to cultivate a deep trust in the self, in "one's ability to come through the trauma–recovery sequence, and experience one's own generative capacity. Gradually one's experiential reach is able to encompass blends of intrusiveness/obtrusiveness/abandonment/support that is part of all 'inter'-'subject'ivity." (Eigen, 2004, p. 34).

For the Bionian Eigen,[53] the rhythm of faith includes the symbolization of affective damage if not catastrophes, "going through the murderous object that psychic birth evolves – as process of opening the worst and coming through." (2004, p. 34). Included here is the ability to "dream" this very catastrophe so as to rework radicalized states of mind.

Eigen's Winnicott allows a rhythm of breakdown↔recovery within and between analyst and analysand as "the individual gets practice in falling apart and coming together, injury and recovery – part of what happens when two humans beings are together" (2004, p. 57) and "my approach to therapy became galvanized by such experiences: to stay open to the impact of the other, whatever gets set off, follow the impact through its transformations, stay with it, and stay with it some more. Impact (shock waves) gives rise to feelings, to images, to thoughts, to … an ever undulating series of states involving unconscious transmission, imaginative visions, and reflective communications." (2004, pp. 58–59). Within the rhythm of faith, one finds in all of Eigen's case studies (1992, 1995) an ability, if not need, to remain *being-with* the Other in such a way that tolerating and transforming primal agonies, our primordial despair, if not primordial doubt, becomes possible. *Being-with* (allowing the Other into one's "psychic bloodstream") in a rhythm of faith brings to pass a waking dream narrative (Bion's+Y) of the analysand's conscious and unconscious wounding object, nursing the inviolable I into life. Despite such a powerful rhythm able to *reimagine* and *reignite* psychic growth after it has been exposed to wounding experiences, Eigen adds his own analytic gift in sensitively applying the rhythm of faith, reflecting his own unique and creative mending/bonding potential:

A therapist may or may not get the message, but he tries to stay with the situation until it begins to reach him. To talk about reaching the patient before the therapist is reached can be premature. The therapist speaks from a place he is touched, which includes his own incomplete, ongoing bonding process, with its incessant dream-work … As a therapist, it is necessary to go even deeper into strangulated states – *not only to observe*, but *to feel* the closing in on oneself, collapsing, enduring mutilation, becoming aware of rotten, ruptured areas of one's own life. … [But] often one finds damage to self, tied to embedded damaged objects that are now part of self. It is not possible to remove the damage to self by removing the damaged object[54] (e.g. residues of a depressed or psychotic or abusive parent): the damage is done. But one can help a person to open new channels to process the damage, enabling new states of self to evolve.

(Eigen, 2001a, pp. 3–4)

In conclusion, Eigen's *rhythm of faith* includes the symbolization of affective damage, "going through the murderous object that psychic birth evolves – as process of opening the worst and coming through" (2004, p. 34), the reworking of radicalized states of mind and body (T-ego and body-ego), not through entropy and de-linking, but by being truthful within our destructiveness, our catastrophes, and our capacity to be more.

Notes

1   Experienced Eigen scholars may benefit from reviewing *Coming through the Whirlwind* (1993) and the *Psychotic Core* (1986). Eigen masterfully integrates the "many sparks" of his own depth psychology; Freud's id psychology, Milner's thoughts on "emptiness" and "creativity," Winnicott's approach to unintegration, Ehrenzweig's undifferentiated ego matrix, Matte-Blanco's symmetrical unconscious and the timeless-spaceless unconscious, and Jung's description of "wholeness."

2   See the *Psychoanalytic Mystic* (1998), chapters 1–6, and 12, as well as *The Electrified Tightrope*, Introductory Notes (pp. xvii–xxvii) and Afterword (pp. 259–278).

3   For such a micro-reading or micro text, see sections titled "The Taint" and "The Split" in *Psychic Deadness* (1996, pp. 102–104).

4   Also review E. Neumann's *Origins and History of Consciousness* (1954/1999), E. Balint's *Before I was I* (1993), and J. Grotstein's *Dual Track Theorem* (1981, 1997).

5   For scholars interested in Eigen's unique Elkin touch, see *The Psychotic Core* (1986, pp. 57–59).

6   Also review "Concerning rebirth. 1. Forms of rebirth" in C. Jung, *Collected Works of C. G. Jung*, Vol. 9, Part 1. 2nd ed. Princeton, NJ: Princeton University Press, 1968, pp. 113–115. Five different forms of rebirth are discussed: Metempsychosis, reincarnation, resurrection, renovation, and witnessing/partaking in a rite of transformation. See the cases of Frank and Carl in Eigen (1986, pp. 87–99).

7   "The eyes of shame," in Ayers (2003, chapter 1, p. 31) reviews Leon Wurmser's work on the archaic drives, drives which are evidenced at birth, i.e., theatophilia and delophilia – the desire to watch, observe and merge (T-ego) as well as the desire to express oneself (body-ego) and be experienced as the object of fascination; "Wurmser postulates that the core of one's self-concept and object world is formed by *theatophilia and delophilia*" (Ayers, 2003, p. 31).

8   Eigen's discussion on "the problem of differentiation" in *The Electrified Tightrope* (1993, pp. 57–59), serves as succinct summary of Elkin's conceptualizations under consideration in this section.

9 Also review chapters 4 to 7 in Ayer (2003): "The Evil Eye and the Great Mother," "The Eyes of the Terrible Mother," "The Look," and "The Eyes of Love."

10 See the work of Keri Cohen in Fuchsman et al. (2021, chapter 3).

11 See Eigen (2001b, p. 27), for a beautiful description on the importance of our inner and outer face. The mirror (as stage), as in the work of Lacan and others, mainly focus on the shock of reality and the denial of the Real. Eigen adds however, that the outer face, the face in the mirror, also *supports a coming through* a warped inner face/experience/feel. Eigen's work allows a dialectic rather than a *singular view.*

12 I could not help thinking here of St. Teresa of Avila and her work, the *Interior Castle.*

13 Review Wolfgang Giegerich (2020, p. 37) for a description wherein Jung's cures a patient after a single session (of insomnia) by singing an old lullaby. Also review Vamik Volkan's ideas on the voice (1976, 1995).

14 Eigen in M. Winborn's *Shared Realities* (2014), pp. 130–143, and in *Faith* (2014b), chapter 7.

15 See Federn's "I feel" in both the *Psychotic Core* (1986) and *Coming through the Whirlwind* (1993). Eigen mentions in a footnote (1986, p. 85, n. 55) that American psychoanalysis might have developed very differently had Federn's ego psychology won over Hartmann's ego psychology. We may hope for a growing Federn–Hartmann dialectic in time.

16 See Marguerite Sechehaye's *An Autobiography of a Schizophrenic Girl* (1951), especially chapters 13 to 16.

17 Ofra Eshel's work is of immense importance here. See, chapters 2, 6, 7, 8–10, in *The Emergence of Analytic Oneness* (2019).

18 The reader may also review Eigen's "The Corrupt Body Self" (pp. 314–320) as well as "The Corrupt Mental Self" (pp. 320–322) in *The Psychotic Core* (1986).

19 See Eigen's writing on "Omnipotence and omniscience" in *The Psychotic Core* (1986).

20 See the case of Arnie in *Feeling Matters* (2007) describing "trauma clots". The theme is reviewed in *Under the Totem* (2016, pp. 51–54), integrating Elkin's T-ego and body- ego splits with Bion's *Tower of Babble.* Daniel, an analysand in *Under the Totem,* compliments Arnie's descriptions, i.e., the importance and need of *rebirth imagery* (Eigen in Fuchsman et al., 2021, chapter 1), Elkin's *resurrection potential.*

21 See "Abstinence and the schizoid ego" (chapter 1, 1993), again discussed under "Light" (2007), especially pages 67–71, and *Ecstasy* (2001b), p. 98.

22 See Marian Campbell's chapter "Psychic aliveness: on 'being murdered into life'" (in Bloch & Daws, 2015, chapter 6).

23 Various cases in *The Psychotic Core* (1986) come to mind; Leila (pp. 163–168), Smith (pp. 186–189), Paul (pp. 189–197), Dee (pp. 192–195), and Ellie (pp. 196–198) to name a few.

24 See the case of Milton in *Damaged Bonds* (2001a, chapter 4, pp. 70–75) wherein Eigen writes on "a place (or no- place) where he cannot expel horror … Horror collapses in on itself, and no alpha function can keep up with it. Experiencing alpha function/dream work's insufficiency is a start. As I often say, something gets through, something changes" (p. 75).

25 See Elkin (1972, pp. 403–405), for a detailed discussion.

26 See James Grotstein's *Memory of Justice* (1987, pp. 69–70).

27 Chapter 7 of *The Psychotic Core* (1986) as well as Eigen's case books (1992, 1995) provide accessible guideposts and examples of such receptivity.

28 The case of Milton, pp. 51–54, in *Ecstasy* (2001b) comes to mind, as well as Eigen's *Lust* (2006a).

29 See Elkin (1972, pp. 412–414), for a more in-depth description.

30 This reads close to Bion's links in the *container-contained* either being commensal, symbiotic, or parasitic.

31 See Eigen's area of the *unit self's psychic webspinning*, in *The Electrified Tightrope* (1993), pp. 110–117.

32 For Winnicott: "The most aggressive and therefore the most dangerous words in the languages of the world are to be found in the assertion I AM" (in *Home is Where we Start from*), as well as "Now I want to say: 'After being – doing and being done to. But first, being.'" (in *Playing and Reality*).

33 Michael Balint's "Area of creation," in *The Basic Fault* (1968), and Enid Balint's *Before I was I* (1993), chapter 3, "On being empty of one self," can be read with Eigen's Winnicott.

34 Eigen's case on Leila serves as an educative moment; "The distinction-union ('I am but am not my body; I am but am not my mind; I am but am not my …') was not lost in her illness … She became one with therapy … Yet she never gave in to therapy either … Her envy functioned both to differentiate and to unite us … It is as if she was saying, '*We ought to be one but we are not. We're different. We ought to be different but we're not. We're one.*' … The forms this doubleness-oneness assumes may, at times, be circuitous and hidden. However, as can be seen in Leila's case, psychotic processes *exploit rather than dispense* with this basic structure" (1986, p. 166).

35 See the case of Lauren, in *Ecstacy* (2001b, pp. 44–45) for a succinct discussion of Grotstein's concept of the background subject-object of primary identification.

36 See part IV, chapters 1–10, and the various instructive diagrams, in Winnicott's *Human Nature* (1988).

37 See Eigen's *Rage* (2002)

38 For Eigen's unique description of Freud's creativity see *The Electrified Tightrope*, chapter 15 (pp. 177–180).

39 See especially Eigen's *The Psychotic Core* (1986), chapters 1–3, and 8, as well as chapters 7–9 in the *Electrified Tightrope* (1993).

40 Eigen, "The core sense of creativeness that permeates transitional experiencing is reborn on a new level, insofar as *genuine not me nutriment becomes available for personal use.* (1993, p. 112; emphasis added). An in-depth discussion concerning rebirth as defined by Eigen and Winnicott's notion of "The life of an individual is an interval between two states of unaliveness" (Winnicott, 1988, p. 132) may prove fruitful in future work.

41 Job 13:15, King James Version; "Though He slay me, yet will I trust in Him: but I will maintain mine own ways before Him. He also shall be my salvation."

42 See Dunne (2015, pp. 221–223).

43 Also see Eigen (1999) chapters 9 and 10; (2004), chapter 2, and (2005), chapter 3.

44 Eigen's reading on Winnicott's concept *primary aloneness* can be found in the first two chapters of *Flames from the Unconscious: Trauma, Madness and Faith* (2009).

45 See chapter 9, "Shadows of agony X" in *Toxic Nourishment* (1999), and Eigen's *own crib talk* and sensitivity to time, 1999, chapter 2 (also in 2007).

46 Eigen's discussion on Winnicott's use of *unintegration* in the *Psychotic Core* (1986, pp. 331–348) could be read in tandem with Winnicott's x+y+z conceptualization. Eigen also makes creative links with the importance of *Unintegration* and the capacity to dream, work later combined with Bion in describing damaged dream-work and the *undreamable object* (chapters 3 and 4 in *Damaged Bonds*, 2001, pp. 43–75).

47 Also evident in Eigen's *The Psychotic Core* (1986). Review pp. 334–335 for a differentiation between "the rest of the *Baby Soul*," unintegration, and later disintegration (i.e. the formation of defenses, even encysted self-object units, as the infant progresses through developmental phases à la Elkin, 1972).

48 A. Watts (1989, 2009).

49 See Eigen's later work on *sanitizing processes* in society (in *Toxic Nourishment*) as well as Bollas's normotic pathologies.

50 Phenomenologically, Eigen's *Psychotic Core* (1986, p. 126) synoptically refers to the psychology of mindlessness and "quickening processes," as well as the phenomenology of "functional speed differences."

51 Recall Eigen's description of Bion's analytic bearing.

52 For a beautiful comparison between Bion's O and Milner's O see the *Psychoanalytic Mystic* (1998), p. 77.

53 Also review Eigen (2004), p. 31, and Day 3, "Morning session: murder and coming through," pp. 55–73, in Eigen (2010) for an in-depth discussion on Bion's notion of being murdered into life.

54 See in an upcoming chapter "Sarah's tree."

Part II

Clinical Eigen

We need to learn to speak inside the storm. To hear storm's voice ... How to speak from inside affectively, to let affect speak. To be the affect speaking for a time. Not totally, always, or absolutely- that would be as impossible as it is undesirable. We are a mixture of distance-immersion, contact–disengagement, connection-disconnection ... I might add respectful, caring contact – contact that cares for experience. Contact that cares for sensing what is happening to us.

(Eigen, 2004, p. 219)

DOI: 10.4324/9781003002871-5

Clinical Elger

Chapter 4

The psychotic core and coming into being

Eigen's primordial horizon

> My use of phenomenology is informal and hybrid. It aims at bringing out
> aspects of psychological events that may evoke a more profound awareness
> of psychic reality … *My goal is less 'explanation' than appreciation and the
> growth personal encounter brings.*
>
> (Eigen, 1986, pp. 83–84)

Introduction

Eigen's original clinical psychoanalytic writings can be read in depth in the
beautifully edited work by Adam Phillips titled *The Electrified Tightrope* (1993).
Although *The Electrified Tightrope* was published after Eigen's *Psychotic Core*
(1986), it is essential to engage in a psychoanalytic reverie concerning Eigen's
central themes, starting as early as 1973. According to Phillips, Eigen's work
between 1973–1993 can be summarized as follows:

> It is the capacity to experience, for the therapist and the patient both, how
> it can be sustained, and the diverse and subtle ways it can be sabotaged
> that is the absorbing preoccupation of Michael Eigen's remarkable psy-
> choanalytic essays.
>
> (Phillips, 1993, p. xiii)

The analyst and analysand's capacity to experience, sustain, and remain in
contact with the primordial dimensions of experience and the various diverse
and subtle ways the latter may be circumvented are phenomenologically
explored in no less than *seven focus areas* between 1973[1] and 1990.[2] Eigen's
early essays describe the clinical care of patients communicating vexing states
of mind – forms and processes explained in greater depth in the *Psychotic
Core* (1986) and *Psychic Deadness* (1996), as well as two clinical works of
psychotherapeutic art, *Coming through the Whirlwind* (1992) and *Reshaping
the Self* (1995). Principally, psychoanalytic themes of importance to Eigen are
the primordial "levels" of psychic pain that contemporary clinicians define
as the *area of the basic fault* (Balint, 1968). Despite the most obvious realities

DOI: 10.4324/9781003002871-6

found in the *area of the basic fault*, Eigen's psychoanalytic sensibility maps untapped creative aspects of pathology (1973–1974). Initial writings include "Abstinence and the schizoid ego," and "The recoil of having another person," both in 1973, both focusing on dangerous yet restorative aspects in regression, as well as distance–closeness dimensions in psychoanalysis treatment. "Psychopathy and individuation" published in 1975, followed by a transformative paper articulating *psychic distaste*[3] in the Other, titled "Working with unwanted patients", explore the reality of "self-affirmative aspects of acting out" (1977, in 1993, p. xvii) and the therapeutic use of the therapist's negative states. Staying with, tolerating, and transforming that which is unwanted is clinically thickened by various probes into the psychoanalytic significance of the face, the importance of ideal images, the need for faith and paradox, all between 1979 and 1982. A truly transformative period in Eigen's writing is characterized by a *refinding* of *that which was already evident* in well-known theorists whose writings were "such *intensely alive affirmations of the human spirit in adversity* ... Winnicotts' concern with feeling unreal, Bion's with psychic deadness, Lacan with self-deception – yet all demonstrated a passionate striving for Truth beyond reach; *all were excited by evolution of self.*" (in 1993, p. xx; emphasis added). The "I-yet-not-I" and the "Sense of creativeness" in 1983 all predate "Demonized aspect of the self" (1984, in 1993) and introduce a central concept throughout Eigen's oeuvre described as *union and differentiation*, later the *distinction–union structure*. Also, in this period, Eigen refocused the centrality of creativity in both Freud's and Winnicott's work, and explored two demonic-like networks in the personally, i.e., an *explosive-fusional body ego* and a *mocking-controlling covertly transcendent mental ego,*[4] expanding the work of Henry Elkin in many ways.

In "Between catastrophe and faith" (1985) and "Omnipotence, mindlessness-selflessness, and omniscience" (1986–1989, in Eigen, 1993), Eigen clinically traces the myriad of ways in which patients may dismantle their attention and mind, blank out, and rely on vanishing points, all in service of escaping various body-ego and T-ego catastrophes. In essence, "*Omnipotence* can be related to *vicissitudes of body self* and *omniscience to mental self*, with every variety of mixture and conflict." (1993, p. xxvii). The analytic probes read phenomenologically rich and are furnished with surprisingly accessible technical considerations for the clinician. Eigen relates as passionately and deeply to psychoanalytic theory as to the analysand and his own reveries. In doing so, what arises is a testament of Eigen's singular orphic psychoanalytic mind and the beginning of his well-known concept: a rhythm of faith approach.

On the apperception of a radiant I-point

To return to 1973, Eigen starts his psychoanalytic writing describing the importance of "abstinence" as part of a revolutionary capacity within the self and culture to offset "toxic elements" evident in both. Against the backdrop of the abstinence rule, as found in general analytic praxis, Eigen envisions abstinence as reflecting *a deeper primordial need* (Eigen's incommunicado self/ cosmic I/inviolable I?) for an *abstinence spot* (*sabbath point of soul* in later work) between Id and Superego realities, an area able to give rise to an aesthetic moment for transformation. Eigen mentions, in *Faith*, that if the analytic pair could *hold out*↔ *hold in* within the abstinence spot, something new, if not transformative, may arise.[5] Eigen would return to this theme in "Boa and flowers" (1996, chapter 18) with his analysand Janice many years later in greater detail, exploring difficulties evident when such aesthetic invitations are left unanswered. Where it is possible, new psyche-beginnings are indeed possible. An analysand of Eigen called Kurt, in contrast to Janice, reflected on the abstinence spot as follows; "He [Kurt] called it an 'infusion of life, spirit, feeling'. Deeply passive nourishment, an 'infusion of life'" (2011, p. 92).

Clinically, Eigen also gently introduced the reader to a most painful reality, that those traumatized by external reality may find the abstinence spot both needed *and* dangerous. That is, for analysands disillusioned with/by the outer world, inwardness and indwelling "toward a barely sensed ego experience" (1993, p. 5) might naturally be invoked, but in turn, evoke cosmic panic, a dread of disintegration, and a sense of catastrophic emptiness, if not void.[6] More than a cacoon transference at work during such states of being. Similar to Guntrip and Winnicott, Eigen views such indwelling as reflecting agonies that could find both alloplastic and autoplastic adaptations, including schizoid withdrawal, psychopathy, and even delinquency. Despite these well-known "reactions" to deprivation, if not privation, Eigen creatively expands and articulates other possibilities within psychoanalytic presencing. In Eigen's vision, emptiness can be found enlivening, even full, and psychopathy may even hold signs of individuation! Eigen's personal maturational sensitivities and history, as well as Elkin's influence, serve as creative backdrop to unseen and more profound possibilities. One could certainly imagine that many of our mind-body's reactions to illness are related to the mind-body's actual attempt to cure and heal itself from disease and infection (a T-ego and body-ego *wu wei*?). This logic seems evident in Eigen's approach to the psyche and thoughts on abstinence, i.e., our *autochthonous creative regenerating inwardness*, as described above, can support the analysand to both experience and unite with an underlying indestructible sense of self, evoking contact and knowledge of an inviolable core sense able to be put to creative psychoanalytic use (Eigen's apperception of a radiant I-point or kernel):

> sighting and uniting with an ego structure which is experienced as the underlying indestructible sense of self – a compressed, dense, magnetic I–kernel, a seeming final contracting point of the I ... It is as though the discovery and exploration of the safety zone of the I – an *inviolable*

I within a hidden enclosure – makes possible the generosity which allows the other to become genuinely attractive.

(1993, p. 5; emphasis added)

Eigen creatively holds that such an indwelling to the self's safety zone, a psychic homecoming of sorts, can be experienced as more than the *passive regressed schizoid ego* as found in the work of Harry Guntrip, and may *reignite* the inherent capacity to experience intrinsic goodness in *"Be" –"ing"* in the world (Winnicott's I AM). Reigniting the autochthonous self frees the flow of libido to be *reinstituted*, reinstating a "two-way current of outflow and inflow" (1993, p. 5). The following may serve as an example of such experiencing from the 1973 publication:

Analysand A: There was a sliver there, black and radioactive, compressed and dense ... the very bottom ... It was what was *unbreakable* in me ... the *uncracked kernel* ... only *that* survived everything.

(1986, p. 2; emphasis added)

Analysand Carl: It stands in one place ... like a light tower or a bridge, dense stone ... black space endlessly around it ... I want to touch and break it because it won't give an inch ... but I'll break before it will ... as though I am breakable and it's not ... *I want to unite with it and make it the part of me it is….* It's more than me ... *the I-ness of my I.*

(1986, p. 4; emphasis added)

Eigen expands on the notion of a radiant I kernel in describing the treatment of an alcoholic analysand (Abe), becoming increasingly regressed and withdrawn in therapy. Eigen writes that, in containing his own growing anxiety and fear for the analysand's state of mind, Eigen found the analysand able to touch upon this safety zone in himself, supporting a re-engagement with both Eigen and the world at large.[7] As Eigen artfully illustrates, this movement was more than a *regressed ego coming to life*, the baby in the drawer in need of therapeutic ministration à la Guntrip. *It is the language and area of the inviolable I.* Eigen's inviolable I also differs from Winnicott's sacred core of selfhood, the never-to-be-invaded or impinged by the outside world core, as *Eigen's inviolable I cannot be impinged upon in the way classical analysts view the True Self.* It is *"that in me which is safe from all harm"* (1993, p. 7), safe from being collectivized in Elkin's language. An analysand named Pete (see Daws, in Bloch and Daws, 2015, pp. 115–125), brought this to life when he mentioned that "as a *child of God*, I cannot be extinguished, we cannot be extinguished," and read to me, emotionally so, the well-known poem by William Ernest Henley (written 1875) titled *Invictus*, accentuating the reality of "our unconquerable soul." In Eigen's own description,

Therapy supported a situation – blindly, mutely – in which Abe's psyche, in *conjunction with mine*, created a sequence wherein beginnings were sustained and led to something creative (sustaining is itself creative). *One of the most creative moments of all was apperception of a radiant I point that lifts existence.* This experience occurred unexpectedly in a situation of extreme abstinence and contraction.

(2011, p. 9; emphasis added)

Eigen furthers his active "waiting"[8] (1993, p. 12) in exploring the outward flow of dissociated psychopathic tendencies into the whole of personality, personalities that are primarily non-psychopathic. Similar to Winnicott (1984), Eigen believes in creating a psychic space and understanding, if not *waiting*, to consider the importance of *psychopathy on, or even as, individuation*! Nietzsche's "psychopathic vital streak (spark?)" (1993, p. 9) is frequently short-circuited, relegated to dissociated parts, or left to the domain of thoughtless acting in/out. Id and ego destroying superego short-circuit the developmental spark the so-called antisocial impulse may bring (Chrzanowski, 1973). It is indeed challenging to allow Romulus and Remus their wolf-play. As such, Eigen mentions that the psychopathic vital streak certainly has frightening content but also "curative aim" (1986, p. 12), adding, "It (the psychopathic vital streak) grew and receded with its own natural rhythm or sense of time which included or in some way took into account the therapist's own pace or rhythm" (1993, p. 12). As with schizoid tendencies, the dissociated psychopathic tendencies can "receive integration by central or communal ego structure" (1993, p. 11), a reminder that self-awakening occurs on different levels of meaning and developmental stages. A stunning example can be found in Rose-Emily Rothenberg's work (2001) in discussing an extramarital relationship and its transformative impact on the process of her psychosomatic healing process (from keloids, pp. 63–65). Moralistic approaches may mainly see compliance and passivity without enlivened integration and further growth to self and care for the other. Daseinanalyst Todd Du Bose (2020) mentions that the psychopathic vital streak is frequently found in the Old Testament as the initial step to spiritual transformation, meeting and accepting God, and needing abysmal consolation. Closer to Eigen's work, a central concern to Winnicott is his notion that delinquency can be held as a last-ditch effort at contact and attachment (1984). One could also read the touching work of Franz Fanon's rage in this way – a need to break through, into, and make soul contact (Eigen's *Rage*, 2002). It has been a central concern for Eigen, later thickened in cultural works such as *Flames from the Unconscious* (2009), *The Age of Psychopathy* (2006c), as well as the three Seoul volumes (2010, 2011, 2021). Severed nerve-endings have immense consequences for communal ego development. Despite the latter, and its daimonic underlay, Eigen holds that *dosage* may be needed, titration a must, given the analysand and his or her psychic and social environment. Eigen's psychanalytic cases[9] are beautiful reminders of a psychoanalyst attempting to "nurse a storm" (p. 15), "feeling my fingers ... on the pulse of the storm ... though I could not control it I had some influence inside it" (1993, p. 15). This reads similar to the breathtaking work of Ofra Eshel's "I will go with you!"[10] (see Eshel in Bloch and Daws, 2015, chapter 9), in true psychoanalytic faith. Not only do schizoid and psychopathic patients reflect their own category of difficulty, but so do those deemed *Unwanted* (Eigen, 1977, in Eigen, 1993). Psychic distaste, naturally evoked by interactions characterized by overcloying and obnoxious negativism (acting hostile-dependently) and cynicism, all create an atmosphere of muted rage and resentment.

> Their identity is formed by a chronic sense of injury together with a *primitive union* with the phallic mother – male or female – who injured them ... Their personality deformations, further, frequently express themselves in physically unappealing ways, such as unkept obesity or severely distorted facial and postural rigidities. In these cases the *actual body* has become closely identified with and formed by a negative self-image.
>
> (1993, p. 25)

The body-ego here serves as evidence of the exposure to damaged bonds and toxic nourishment. Unwanted, undreamt, their psycho-physical distortions reflect, in Stanley Keleman's language, the *emotional insults on the human form* (1989). Eigen traces the constricting distortion of insults (Eigen's impact language within a distinction–union structure) in shock, abuse, neglect, and trauma. Shock and freeze shape and activate mind–body splits as mentioned. Trauma implies too much or too little, a rupture and tear, impacting tissue – a muscular-skeletal armoring. Abuse leads to irritation, wearing down and feeling worn down, inflammation, even exhaustion. Neglect is equated to atrophy, indifference to mind-body-self and others. Combining the latter with denial and externalization, fruitful dialogue about inner life remains primarily foreclosed. The therapeutic field becomes increasingly filled with an atmosphere too thick or thin to breathe, seeing the analysand, even analyst, developing an *emotional black lung*. The somatic-emotional breakdown in "be"-ing unwanted provokes interpersonal and therapeutic recoil, distaste, frustration, even non-involvement. The unwanted patient, similar to the schizoid, psychopath, and the entrenched, brings to therapy a fundamental relational logic: despite resentment and protestation, true contact remains dangerous, and therapist hopping may prove a successful way of protecting the self from engulfment or being "dropped." "Stopping" the patient to settle down will carry its risks and rewards; "It is as though there exists a quota of distance which must be fulfilled and spontaneous fluctuations in the balance of the power to conspire to ensure that space" (1993, p. 27).

Treating and remaining faithful to the analysand that evokes dislike remains essential to the psychoanalytic pair's developmental rhythms. Developing sensitivity, psychic tastebuds for the *range and dosage* of the bitter and hostile remains challenging. As most would attest, staying the analytic course in time may support something to grow; dislike may turn to more subtle forms of psyche taste and tasting, small variation suddenly seem possible, and life-giving nourishing variations (Eigen's *basic love*) may be relied upon.

> As the therapist consciously lives through this vicious circle enough times, he begins to telescope and develop increasing control over its negative impact …he reduces the intensity of dislike or distaste a patient can invoke in him … he becomes more sensitive to the *various nuances of negative feelings the patient can stimulate, and his interventions become more highly differentiated* … the therapist learns to modulate *his show in liking* in a way *that fits the patient's ability to process positive feelings* [!]. As the therapist develops an accurate trust in himself, his contact with his sense of *basic love* becomes more constant *but is appropriately tempered and adapted to the patient's need for hate and distance*.
>
> (1993, pp. 27–28; emphasis added)

Eigen's *basic love approach* also supported the evolution of alienation's underlying dialectics in the visual sphere of holding (mind-ego), not just taste (body-ego). With Elkin as background, both the mind-eye and mouth-nipple nourish each other in their own distinction–union structure ways (*T-ego* and *body- ego*). That is, as with Elkin's thinking, the primordial mouth-nipple contact stands in a developmental relationship with the visual-mind ego (see Chapter 3). For Eigen, we all have visual taste buds too! In articles published in 1979–1982, Eigen explores the dialects of alienation, the non-communal adaptations as suffering from, as a patient of mine termed it, being exposed to an *optic rectomitis* (critical eyes, mocking face, negative gaze). As with later work, both the mind-ego and body-ego have taste preferences and difficulties that fall victim to either Balint's ocnophilic or philobatic adaptations (Balint, 1968). Hungry eyes meet evacuative eyes [11] (see Eigen, 2001a, pp. 59–61), a retentive or encapsulated body meets somatic leakage and purging (Eigen, 2001a, p. 133), vacant eyes may reflect a ravenous hungry mouth and withholding body. Variations are infinite!

Furthermore, similar to Winnicott's notion of paranoid and non-paranoid adjustments to the environment, Eigen writes that the *original pristine ego* may have an essential mixture of paranoid and non-paranoid foundational experiences, the logical product of the I's continuous experience of environmental ministrations. With both Elkin and Spitz, Eigen argues that the infant's initial response to the outside world and its ministrations are essentially non-paranoid; an open inviolable I expanding, both curiously seeing and tasting reality. The smile represents a genuine and non-defensive response to the world, worlding, or environing, as no dissociation between thinking-feeling-action has yet occurred. Given the complexity of maternal ministration, the impact of being with the Other will see a crisis in the ego's foundational freedom and openness, given the growing awareness of power and power inequalities (Elkin's natural values). Eigen again articulates the *area of the inviolable I*, the pre-adaptational and uncompromised I in relation to (a) Kohut's (1971, 1977) mirroring and idealizing processes (the gleam of the mother's eye), (b) Rene Spitz's (1965) genetic view of the adult face provoking a smile response from the infant, and (c) the great Emmanuel Levinas's (1969) birth of the human personality as related to the positive experience of the human face, "For Levinas, the human face gives rise to a sense of the Infinite in relation to which one can become inexhaustibly real" (Eigen, 1993, p. 55). Eigen sculpts a kind of visual field (eye-mind)-tactile field (mouth-mind) co-creation, serving as the basis for the concept *differentiation–union*.[12] In this co-creation, Eigen addresses the tendency for psychoanalysis to equate the breast with the face, whereas for Eigen, given Elkin, each should be treated as a crucial psychic reality in its own right,[13] an untapped psychoanalytic contribution from Eigen. As an alcoholic analysand remarked to Eigen, "my face before I got shit faced," or another, "I saw a baby drink in soul from her mother's eyes … my soul glanced off my mother's eyes. Her eyes were wounding like a weapon" (Eigen, 2006a, p. 98). Kohut's *the gleam of mother's eye* is balanced by French philosophers J. P. Sartre and M. Foucault with their sensitive exploration of the *negative gaze*. The negative gaze, similar to Foucault's panopticism, imprisons the self. The Jungian psychoanalyst S. Wheeley (1992) wrote on looks that kill the capacity for thought, beautifully describing the *anti-life object* in Fordham's theory of deintegration-reintegrative processes; Narcissus and Echo (Wurmser's drives) entwined in a diminished, diminishing dialectic, reflecting a lack of reciprocity, self-agency, tenderness, and care. Could the visual-mental I be more critical than the body-ego I, or the inverse? Is the reflection of Narcissus a non-embodied visual-I "staring" back at the embodied Narcissus, in turn, staring into his reflection as a lost non-reflective I? Could the "staring" reflect a desperate search for oneness and wholeness with self or the Other, or an attempt to integrate the visual-mind I and the body-ego I? Falling into the area of non-integration, drowning even, may serve a much-needed transitional medium for rebirth, finding a more wholesome mind-body I? It should not be forgotten that Narcissus was born, not from a tender union, but from sexual violence, his father a river god. How curious then, as an adolescent, for the very first time, to lose himself in an image reflected in the very substance of his "god" father.

> *Analysand on the paternal gaze:* My father criticized all I did, everything, never good enough, shit. His eyes turned all to shit, bummed me out. He had optic rectomitis!

Analysand on the maternal gaze: I feel inside myself that I look good, in my mind's eye I see myself, and I am fine, I feel good only until I see myself in the mirror. The inside I and the visual I are not the same – I am shocked. How can they be so different! Ugly, old, cannot stand it. My eyes? My mother's eyes? *My* mother eyes? Mother's eyes of my body imperfection are more than my eyes of my imperfection?[14]

It should also be mentioned that the mirror may balance inner warps of self-feel,

Eigen: There are moments like these when I look in the mirror and my actual face doesn't look nearly as bad as my face in inner vision. "That's not so bad," I say to myself. My face looks strong, together, not falling apart or warped. Somehow I feel better, snap back to myself. Seeing my face in the mirror gives me a sense of unexpected relief and cohesion. I come together again, feel just plain me, saved by the image in the mirror. At such a moment, the image in the mirror makes me real.

(Eigen, 2001b, p. 27)

Didn't both Echo and Narcissus pine for physical-visual love only to lose their bodiliness? Echo's disembodied voice, body-I, meet similar processes in Narcissis's transformation after drowning (death of the body and mind-I, i.e., rebirth?). Body and visual/mental I are built up in time and highly susceptible to the mother and father's still-face (water-reflection), emotional blindness, evacuative gaze (Eigen, 2001a, see p. 59), and emotional keratosis.[15] This visual and spoken word is *not me* (a personification, *soul blindness, soul murder*). The self's journey remains fraught with visual-body dangers – myths such as Medusa[16] and Oedipus are constant companions to the *visual/mind-body self*. If you cannot "see," you may be physically and mentally annihilated.[17] If mother and father cannot see or contain, as in physical-emotional holding, annihilation anxieties abound. Psychoanalysis is aptly referred to as *insight orientated*;

Eigen on a recovering schizophrenic woman: One can lose the face of the other as an organizing frame and try to pitch battle in other domains. For example, a recovering schizophrenic woman: "Eat is part of death. Ear is part of hear. Eat is part of hear. I got ear infections before I was a year from my mother's inability to hear. She couldn't let me in. She felt me by plunging into me. The sound of her plunged into me. I tried to shut her sound out. Hearing terrified me. I shut her out so much I feared going deaf. I am excruciatingly sensitive … Yet I shut life out. I am deaf. You penetrate me all over. You spread through me like liquid. I shut you out. My body is an ear that does not hear. They say you can't keep sound out: you can, you *can.*" In her case, vision was eclipsed by a battle with sound, scarred and dissolved by conflict over hearing … Hearing can eat you up, spread everywhere, unmodulated by vision.

(Eigen, 2006a, p. 99)

Eigen further explores the latter annihilation anxieties in both *T-ego and body-ego* compromises in works titled *Omnipotence, Mindlessness-Selflessness, and Omniscience* (1985–1989, in Eigen, 1993), a creative period overlapping the publication of *The Psychotic Core* (1986).[18] Eigen traces[19] the kernel f psychosis, the psychotic core, and the psychotic self (subject to a *corrupted* T-ego, body-ego) in minute detail by discussing the impact of T-ego and body-ego splits on the psyche's raw material resulting in (a) hallucinations, (b) mindlessness, (c) compromised boundaries,[20] (d) hate dynamisms, (e) epistemic trauma, and (f) the reliance on psychic reversal.[21] Raw materials of the personality, i.e., thoughts, affects, images, sensations, relationship to self and other, materiality-immateriality, and times-space all form part of Eigen's, Elkin's, Winnicott's, Bions's, Freud's, Jung's (and many others) metapsychology. As psyche material for developmental stages to come, they are relied upon and increasingly integrated as the primordial self develops and adapts. It also becomes evident in Eigen's various psychoanalytic cases[22] that subtle and meaningful differentiation may exist in transcendental ego (hallucinations and thought/thinking delusions) and body-ego (oral-anal-phallic-tactile) madness.[23] Similar to the later works by Armando Ferrari (2004) and Riccardo Lombardi (2017), Eigen introduces the reader to a metapsychological *tour de force* in the *Psychotic Core* (1986) by exploring the most prominent thinkers on psychosis and its main processes; "In some individuals, madness is obvious and the sense of unreality inescapable. In others, it works silently; perhaps it is visible in the gradual erosion of the quality of one's life and the deterioration of the capacity to generate vital and viable meaning" (1986, p. 331); "the psychotic self often lives close to the sense of rebirth" (1986, p. 337). In Eigen's work, madness remains an innate and adaptational reality of both T-ego and body-ego growth traumas in relationship to environing pressures, "Madness is both innate and a form of adaptation. It is a desperate response to emotional pain and the stress of life … it is also part of the way we are innately structured, and it has a developmental timetable of its own." (Eigen, 2004, p. 10).

Furthermore, a compromised distinction–union structure under the sway of a corrupted mental or body self may find a mind speeding up, or slowing down, either transcending or nullifying itself (attacks on linking, black-hole, and white-hole experiences), blurring self–other boundaries (drowning), sensing engulfment and invasion, activating hardening (both endo and exo) processes sealing off various areas of the body-mind. A possible result: believing-feeling-thinking-acting as if one is either a God (schizophrenic transcendental omniscient ego) or live persecuted by God and the devil. A transcendental ego, a corrupted mind-self living as if one has no worlding or body needs (anorexia, or I am somebody if I have a no-body) stands in a complex relationship with a body-ego that becomes, in turn, corrupted and invaded[24] (somatic delusions and hallucinations). The mind-I may feel increasingly unreal, depersonalized, formless, unintegrated, and *influenced*. Although it may read that the two ego's function somewhat separately in my exposition, Eigen argues instead, relying on Tausk's classical 1933 paper "On the origin of the influencing machine in schizophrenia," that there exists a complex interrelationship between, for example, the *mechanized body ego* and the *omniscient megalomanic mental ego*. One could direct, interact, or not, with the other. Given the impact of such realities on thinking (epistemology), reversal remains problematic. That is, there exists a dialectic between mental and body-ego that is both forward and backward moving (between mental-body), "up and/or down" within each ego structure (example oral-anal collapse in the body-ego, or mindlessness/Zero to being a God in the transcendental mental ego) personified in the following Eigen signs; "↔" and "↑↓".[25] The signs have infinite possibilities and results (see Chapter 5), and Eigen provides rich clinical ideas on how to remain buoyant in this area, under the heading "Interventions and the distinction-union structure" (1986, pp. 306–307),[26] as well as comparing Rena's session notes with the mental pain of Judge Schreber (Eigen, 1986, pp. 272–306). Specifically, "My assumption is that a sense of union and distinction pervades all mental action in one or other form and any psychic production can be situated in terms of it" (1986, p. 306). In approaching Rena's quasi-hallucinatory imagery as reflecting a stage of experience, earlier if one will, Eigen touches upon the difficulties in *sustaining spontaneous distinction*. Given the latter, space-time and boundaries may collapse, exposing the self to a primordial confusion and buzzing of the psyche. Waiting and making use of the Other to build vital distinctions (in T-ego and body-ego) is imperative to protect the analysand against further collapse. The following serve as examples.

> *Eigen on distinction*: You have light and darkness all mixed up...You have phallus and penis confused. ... Aren't you speaking as of womb and anus as if they were the same? Are the vagina and anus no different at all?
>
> (1986, p. 308, a body-ego distinction–union intervention)

> *Eigen on mindlessness:* You seem to sink into nowhere for moments, then got out of it with a rich display of imagery. Where were you when you let yourself stop speaking?
>
> (1986, p. 308, transcendental ego differentiation)

> *Eigen with/on Schreber:* You can't tell the difference between God and the Devil ... [touching upon Schreber's ability to die out and be reborn] ... How are we dying out and returning now? And now? And now?[27]
>
> (1986, pp. 308–309)

The T-ego and body-ego distinction-union structure is also discussed in great detail with an analysand called Ruth in *The Psychotic Core* (1986). Ruth confronted analysis with a unique face–womb polarity signifying two kinds of abortive containers. That is, the womb as a source of safety as well as the womb as a source of immense fusional terrors and entombment. The face, in psychic tandem, was needed for stimulation but also the signified darkness.

> *Eigen as face and womb, i.e., multiple open-ended container to Ruth:* How can your face survive my womb? How can your womb survive my face? How can my face survive your womb? How can your face survive your mother's womb? Did your mother have a face? How did your womb and face survive it? How many faces? How many wombs?
>
> (Eigen, 1986, p. 310)

Eigen also mentions various analysands who seem stupefied, seemingly cut off, blanked out, and unable to hear, to be approached with similar logic.

> *Analyst:* I know what pain my speaking may cause you, but I see you are no more comfortable with my silence.
>
> (1986, pp. 310–311)

> *Analysand:* Your words were drops of warm water falling on ice. Each drop made me scream. Words are knives. I'm so tender. I felt you knew that somehow though you continued to speak. I heard the listening in your words at the same time they brushed me aside.
>
> (1986, p. 311)

Reading Eigen, even in *dichotic* and violent destruction, as happened, or as a continual unforgiving moment-to-moment forever happening, the primordial I may remain *alive and able* within its inherent distinction-union capacities and experiences (*neonic freedom*). Despite this truth, Eigen reminds us:

> Tendencies to link together and hold apart permeate our psychic field with variable antagonisms and complementaries. Whatever level or quality of self we touch, the distinction-union structure is there. *And whatever we touch we touch through this structure.* Therapeutic remarks are *rooted* in this foundation, whether willfully or not. The therapist is often called upon to witness the massive mutilation and impoverishment of our most basic feelings and capacities to participate in the (re) constitution of an injured soul from the ground up. He is privileged and challenged to face the requirements of a self that may seem beyond repair. The therapist's own distinction-union *vis-a-vis* the patient in his care will likely be a crucial ingredient in the brew both partners drink or refuse. The sense of self

and *distinction-union grow and die together* ... This *distance-closeness is not something that is "curable." It is an elemental given, our raw material, a condition of our beings.*

(1986, pp. 311–312; emphasis added)

Also, as a concluding thought, reflecting a hopeful attitude in both reaching to, and transforming from, our psychotic selves, Eigen writes:

Throughout our lives we are pregnant with our lives, pregnant with unborn selves and psychic babies, including thoughts, feelings, attitudes, modes of experiencing. A pregnancy that never stops, no matter how many births. *Gestation does not end.*

(Eigen, 2018, p. 44)

Notes

1 An Eigen article frequently overlooked is "The call and the lure" published in 1973.
2 Eigen, in the *Introductory notes* of *The Electrified Tightrope* (1993, pp. xvii–xxviii) divided his phenomenological probes into seven time periods with main concerns.
3 Also see the case of Lea in the *Psychotic Core* (1986), and in *Under the Totem* (Eigen, 2016), pp. 82–84.
4 Integrated with Freud's, Bion's, and Fairbairn's notions of evil. Also see Coleman Nelson and Eigen (1984).
5 Eigen explores his 1973 work in greater details in (2011), chapters 1 and 2. In "Some biographical notes" (in Eigen, 2016), Eigen mentions self-cleansing processes evident in nature, "And I thought of the Taosit *wu wei*. It had not occurred to me the river could be self-cleansing. Life is so often associated with dirty processes, but generative faith runs deeper. It is part of the paradox of living to keep the long view in mind while giving all you have to what you can do now. ... There is more to life than any life can exhaust" (2016, p. 143).
6 Grotstein's Black Hole experience (1981, 2007) and Masterson's Void (1972) come to mind.
7 Also refer to Eigen and Govrin (2007, p. 65) under the section "Light."
8 See also chapter 6 in Eigen (2020), "Beginning to wait and waiting as beginning."
9 See the cases of Tom, Ann, and Ken, in Eigen (1993, pp. 12–18).
10 Eigen's case of Jack remains a beautiful testament to *analytic faith*; "He tells me he's going to kill himself, jump off a bridge, a building. I say I'll jump with, we'll fall and hit the water and ground together. He says over and over, 'You're brave. You're brave. If I were you, I'd lock me away'" (Eigen, 2001b, p. 58).
11 The case of Neil can be reviewed in greater depth in Eigen (2001a, pp. 113–121).
12 As described in chapter 6, "The significance of the face," in Eigen (1993).
13 For an in-depth study see both *The Electrified Tightrope* (1993), pp. 49–104, as well as *The Psychotic Core* (1986), pp. 348–357.
14 Review *Damaged Bonds* (2001), chapters 3 and 4, "Damaged dreamwork" (pp. 43–61) and "The undreamable object" (pp. 62–75). Of special interest to most readers would be "Evacuative eyes" in chapter 3, pp. 59–60.

15 Eigen's transformative paper, "Maternal abandonment threats, mind-body relations and suicidal wishes," *Journal of the American Academy of Psychoanalysis*, 9 (1981): 561–582, is of immense importance here.

16 Eigen adds in *Ecstasy* (2001b), "Yet one *must* see God and Medusa. One must look back. One must approach with urgency. Extremes in experience are necessary. One wants to experience all one can, and use one's equipment to the utmost. Extremes yield the greatest yum" (p. 61).

17 Eigen's "Psychotic self" (in 1986, chapter 8) may be brought into creative dialogue with the work of Vamik Volkan (1995, 1976).

18 See Eigen (1986), p. 329, n. 4.

19 As a reader I remain astounded by not only the content of *The Psychotic Core*, but the scholarly 297 footnotes throughout eight chapters, covering various seminal thinkers in psychoanalysis along with known artists, writers, and the religious traditions.

20 Eigen explores boundaries as related to inside and outside, between object relations, between levels of consciousness, between primary and secondary process, and between mood and affects. Concerning affects also review *Ecstacy* (2001b), *Rage* (2002), *The Sensitive Self* (2004), *Emotional Storm* (2005), and *Lust* (2006a).

21 These areas are synoptically summarized in *The Psychotic Core,* chapter 1, pp. 31–36. Also refer to Eigen (2016), chapter 3, "Fermenting devils in psychosis" (pp. 29–43).

22 See especially the cases of Rena, Frank, and Carl, in *The Psychotic Core* (1986).

23 Growth from recovery from psychosis can be found in Eigen (2011), chapter 7, "Tears of pain and beauty."

24 See the case of Rena, *The Psychotic Core* (1986), pp. 268–282.

25 See Eigen's *The Electrified Tightrope* (1993), chapters 18–20; *Psychic Deadness* (1996), chapter 6, and *Toxic Nourishment* (1999), chapters 7–10.

26 See the dialogue between Lynn and Eigen in *Reshaping the Self* (1995), pp. 66–110, for more examples of Eigen's use of the distinction–union structure.

27 Stunningly activating the psyche's x+y to bind Z.

Chapter 5

Psychic deadness

Scaling mount shock, damaged phantasy pumps, and the need for psycho-dialysis

> Many individuals today seek help because they feel dead. A sense of inner deadness may persist in an otherwise full and meaningful life. Deadness can be related to emptiness and meaninglessness, but is not identical with them. I have seen individuals who are filled with emotions and meaning, but somehow remain untouched by their experiences. They remain *impervious and immune* to the potential richness of what they undergo. They complain of a deadness that persists in the midst of plenty.
>
> (Eigen, 1996, p. xiii)

Introduction

In a transformative work published in 1996, Eigen contemplates and explores the experience of "feeling dead." According to Eigen, the experience of psychic deadness[1] can be understood as a temporary drop in euphoria, be state-like, encapsulated, or reflect a pervasive inner reality. Eigen explores psychic deadness through the lens of various psychoanalysts, most notably Sigmund Freud, Melanie Klein, Sandor Ferenczi, Wilfred Bion, and Donald Winnicott. For the aim of the current volume, special attention will be given to Eigen's thinking on Freud's 1937 writing on man's "obscure inability or resistance to change" (p. xvii), Klein's *destructive force within*, Bion's *no-thing*, Winnicott's *area of freedom,* and Ferenczi's notion of *psychic earthquakes.*

Freud's anti-life found in "unspecified places," and Winnicott's aliveness in an area of freedom

Momentarily suspending the death drive from Freud's psychobiological descriptions and overdetermined focus on the impact of castration anxiety, for Eigen, the "Freudian ego lives a double anxiety." (1996, p. 8). Aliveness-deadness, if not Eros-Thanatos driven experience and thinking, finds libido caught in a double helix. Libido here is conceptualized as being mobile, supporting the ego in both its natural tendency for expansion and adaptation.

DOI: 10.4324/9781003002871-7

In stark contrast, if libido loses its elasticity, becomes rigid (Eigen's psychic rigor mortis), even sticky (Donald Meltzer's adhesive adaptations), the ego may be unable to fight the forces that are against recovery, the *anti-life* objects, introjects, interjects, and environing others. Eigen's Freud also conceptualizes a force that actively fights off recovery, serving as the true kernel of the death instinct, housed in the unconscious, tucked away from our more conscious living. This may read close to Bion's and post-Bionian articulation of the psychotic part of the personality (Civitarese, 2013; Ferro, 2002). Eigen further articulates Freud's appreciation and conceptual capacity to sense the internal and timeless battle for supremacy between maximum aliveness and the organism's tendency toward entropy and deadness (the diminution of psychic energy). Breaking down and falling apart, inertia, exhaustion, collapse, the psyche-body wearing down, all stand in relationship with the psyche's light, vitality, integration, and growth capacities.

> Freud has one eye on mobility, another on barriers. The psyche was alive with pulsating movements. Yet the flow met inner-outer resistances, had its own inertia, stickiness, backflow (regression), and finally emptied in the river of death.
>
> (Eigen, 1996, p. 20)

For Freud, the body-ego (think psychasthenia-neurasthenia, Elkin's body-ego) and our thinking-feeling may all become subject to the organism's maximum and minimum libidinal currents and "investments." Body-mind flooding or barrenness (our full-empty dialectic and hygeiaphrontic reactions) are a daily struggle both qualitatively and quantitatively lived; being too much or too little, thinking-feeling too much or too little, "having" no energy for "doing," or too much explosive energy undoing "doing" (neurasthenia ⇄ mania), and psyche-body rigidity alternating with leakage as in the obsessional neurosis ⇄ hysteria dialectic. Feeling stagnant, flooded, under- or overstimulated all fall under the Freudian vision. Within thinking–feeling immobility, rigidity is akin to death, the kernel of psychical entropy, blocking, and pruning libido and our inherent vitality. As mentioned, older Freud goes deeper, pushing further to a force with deeper roots than superego-ego resistances, found in "unspecified places" (1937, in Eigen, 1996, p. 243). Could this force, a foundational anti-growth tendency, be a foundational human reality? If so, what are the implications? At the risk of theoretical, if not epistemological hopscotch, is this what Harry Stack Sullivan had in mind when he wrote about those *not me* anxieties that remain, in its essence and destructive potentiality, largely inaccessible and unthinkable?

An analysand I will call July, suffering from a variety of debilitating psychosomatic adjustments, described a painful inner feeling, a destructive pull, of "that what damaged me and keeps on damaging me," i.e., being caught in a never-ending deadening compress-decompress gravitational field reminiscent of her affectionately cold and intellectually intrusive parenting.

> They found that some moons around Jupiter shoot ice-like volcanoes – ice volcanoes. Jupiter's moons move elliptically, so when they move away, the gravity loosens a bit. The moons expand, come semi-apart, and fill with *ice-like substance ... They cannot move out too far, as Jupiter's gravitational pull pulls them back* – closer to Jupiter the gravity is so intense the moons are compressed shooting ice, like a volcano! The moons cannot ever escape that massive gravity – and it happens over and over, it is a *timeless compress-decompress movement.*

As a metaphor, a deep anti-life script seems evident, describing both the size and the gravity of her maternal and paternal handling,[2] her inability to be allowed play, to warm up her own libidinal currents due to being swaddled too tightly, literally, and figuratively, with both mother's and father's cold intellect and having to be *the* good, perfect, controlled, and knowledgeable child-adult.[3] Since childhood, July's mind-body, later her potential space, play, thinking, and feeling, collapsed into a psychasthenic spiral governed by rightness, *the* good, and doing good exclusively, squeezing "warming" vitality out of her. The "alteration to the ego" (Eigen, 1986, p. 15) by being exposed to *emotional starvation* (Eigen, 1996, chapter15) and *being too good* (Eigen, 1996, chapter 13) ensured a paradoxical mono-culture; growth is dangerous, the gravity of I AM not known, not wanted, or accepted. Similar to James Masterson's disorders of self triads, most of July's self-activation or coming alive was met with *disaster anxiety* (Eigen, 1996, chapter 16), leading to defense. According to both Eigen and Freud, such alteration remains both structural and atmospheric – even more so,

> Freud pins the warp not in place but in rhythm. The focus here is not psychic topography, but timing and movement. The music of the psyche is off. *A rhythmic rather than a structural warp is crucial.* A rhythmic warp results in structural alterations. Structure depends on rhythms (as well as the reverse).
> (Eigen, 1996, p. 15)

Staying alive despite such a gravitational Thanatos-driven pull and *structural-rhythmic warps* remain a central concern for Eigen's Winnicott. As evident in Chapter 3 of this volume, Eigen's *rhythm of faith* sees the importance of being able to create by *coming against and coming through.* Melanie Klein, Ronald Fairbairn, Margaret Little, and many other psychoanalysts view much of their work based on impassioned pleas for *Being;* for "be"-ing, be-coming, feeling alive, even if needing to *lie fallow.* From Eigen's reading of these thinkers as well as his own unique psychoanalytic sensibilities, the *"movement between is the important moment* [in Winnicott's writing]" (1996, p. 16), as well as the *"movement through"* (1996, p. 16). To creatively, if not spontaneously, move between and through various psychological experiences, especially if the "between," the "liminal," becomes subject to gravitational type rigidities, stagnation, or coagulated trauma globs, thoughts and feelings may, in turn, become subject to timeless primordial traumas. Living "fully" in, and through, an experience becomes foreclosed given our need for survival and adaptation, as "false" as it may be. We are exposed to and can deaden ourselves, our thoughts and feelings in service of surviving.[4]

> *Analysand:* I know I should feel something – there is nothing there where my feeling were – now is just a gap. I don't feel emotions anymore. I can have an image, memories of what accompanies the gap of feeling in me, my lack of heart feelings – I see my mad mother, my enraged crazy father. My feeling self has been damaged, numbed.

Finding a rhythm of faith in the gap may also imply a (growing?) ability to move in and out of a living-death in the distinction–union structure.

The destructive force within: Klein's creative developmental reveries

In stark contrast with the Guntripian womb of safety (Eigen, 1973), the Kleinian womb does not represent rest and respite or a place to withdraw and hide, instead, "The Kleinian womb is a busy place of creativity, power, appropriation, a status symbol" (1996, p. 27). In Eigen's view, *Kleinian deadness* can be ascribed to active mastery attempts gone wrong. Primary anxiety is not linked to libido in the Freudian way but to *a destructive force within.* Object relations exist from the beginning of life, and as such, the self is molded by projection and introjection. More so, from the very beginning, the introjected good breast serves as vital nourishment to ego development, ego-structuring, and affect-vitality. Psychic flow is of the essence (Eigen's ↔). As a digestive and respiratory model, one could imagine psychic dramas based on bad out ↔ good in. Through splitting, projective identification, and introjective identification, that is, Klein' and Eigen's "fantasy pumps" (Eigen, 1996, p. 38), many variations of internal dramas become possible,

> Bad ego can hate bad ego, good ego can love bad ego, bad object can hate good object loving good ego, bad object can love bad ego hating good object, bad object can hate bad ego loving good object, good ego can hate bad ego hating good object, and on and on. This enables mapping of dazzling arrays of *internal-external object-ego-affect relations.*
>
> (1996, p. 31; emphasis added)

Klein's *conflict-anxiety regulatory model* also gives readers a glimpse into an inner life dominated by splitting, as such, finding the dispersal of both negative *and* positive affects as the reason for impoverishing (deadening) the ego.

Affect life may be experienced as disintegrated, in pieces, deadened, depleted, and flat. Eigen creatively and provocatively adds:

> *One holds onto splitting because of its unconscious connection to emotional life.* One multiplies splits in vain attempts to capture or make contact with emotions they disperse. *It may be unclear whether an individual trapped in splitting is trying to recapture or annihilate contact with his emotional life. Usually both are true.*
>
> (1996, p. 32; emphasis added)

For Klein, splitting and dispersal equal death or deadening processes, whereas synthesis equals life, or "recovers aliveness" (1996, p. 32). As such, through active (Kleinian) interpretation, splitting and other defenses should be addressed, creating a much-needed *dispersal cerclage.* To add to Klein's *dispersal cerclage approach*, and similar to Bion, Eigen accentuates that Klein's nuclear destructive force within primarily reflects the ego's reaction to endopsychic destructive processes that remain unknowable – Bion's nameless dread. Dispersal, anxiety (Eigen's disaster anxiety), splitting,[5] and projection-introjection are indeed various ways the ego attempts to manage dread. The overuse of splitting and dispersal deadens the self, although Eigen argues that there are analysands that experience psychic damage so extensively "that splitting is ineffectual or unavailable" (1996, p. 34)! Klein added here those analysands that seem "emotionless" but still held it a variation of anxiety or defense against anxiety. Eigen expands this conceptual and clinical notion and writes that the personality under consideration here may not have followed the path of anxiety as defense – instead, we witness the reality of a damaged psychological capacity to "support emotion."

> It is important to note that in my reformulation, neither side of a polarity (emotionlessness↔anxiety) is made primary at the other's expense. The double arrow expresses the possibility that either *can transform into the other*, or oppose the other, or meld together in various ways. Surely Klein's vision that emotionlessness is a form of anxiety is significant. Much mileage can be gained from understanding deadness as frozen emotion, defense against emotion, emotion in disguise (attacked, denies, split, dispersed emotion). *But such a view can be cruel if the capacity to support emotion is missing or damaged.*
>
> (p. 34; emphasis added)

That is, emotionlessness (feeling dead) takes the place where emotions might have been. Some analysands struggle to generate feelings, sustain emotions, or effectively process emotions once they are experienced. The various works of Joyce McDougall serve as a psychoanalytic testament to such difficulties. Eigen empathically mentions that, for such analysands, it is not so much a "putting together what was split, *so much as creating conditions for growth of capacity*" (1996, p. 34; emphasis added). An analysand, traumatized since early childhood in the most horrific of ways, stated something reminiscent of Eigen's sensitivity after more than five years of twice-weekly session, "Like the song of Van Morrison, *And It Stoned Me* ... for me, I can say, *And It Stoned Me to my Soul* ... Constant harassment and encroachment on my little person, my being ... I am a *lifelong recoverer* now in therapy." As such, Eigen argues for the following:

> An advantage to a more open-ended formulation is that one can consider the possibility of *a relatively defensive or undefensive use of feeling or lack of feeling, depending on the context of the moment* ... both emptiness and anxiety may enliven or denude existence, depending on how they function in a broader psychic context.
>
> (1996, p. 35; emphasis added)

Finally, Klein further accentuates, and Eigen devotes a chapter to this unexpected phenomenon (1996, chapter 13), that excessive goodness may paradoxically serve as the basis for a feeling of deadness! That is, the ego may take refuge from persecution by adhesively latching to an idealized internal object, a marsupial-type attachment needing protection against menacing states. Eigen writes that the more severe the anxiety, the greater the possibility of ego functioning getting thinned by its attempts to ward off ominous states through desperate connections to the idealized (self-other) core; "The ego may experience its loss of functioning as a growing deadness: the ego is really dying" (1996, p. 39). Combined with previous writing on the raw materials found in the psychotic core, it is evident that even idealized states can deplete the ego from needed vitality and a creative sense of self. Similar to Masterson and other object-relations thinkers, it may prove accurate that the idealized introjected or good self-object core gets projected onto/into an external object, and in the process, the psyche experiences a deadening sense due to a slow and insidious depletion of inner goodness (the waning of True Self and being eclipsed by False Self adaptations). Immutable deadening variations are possible. Only the object can be good; thus, one's own sense of good remains at the mercy of the other's reflection – a defensive type of ego-bloodletting in a desperate attempt to survive. Also, as only the object is experienced as good, the destructive inner force slowly creeps and annexes the emptied inner core. The inner self is left depleted, under siege, and may be unable to create or access autochthonous learning, or just be – a truly impoverished state of inner life; i.e., the inner self may become megalomanic, inflated, filled with magical ideas:

> The magical world is simultaneously an ideal place and a nightmare: one cannot learn or grow; one is damned to live in an eternal, static,

directionless present. Bion interpreted a patient's fearful use of magical thinking by saying, "What a shame it is that you have been reduced to omnipotence."

(Ogden, 2009, p. 95)

Bion's no-thing, keeping the unknown open, and the catastrophe machine

Possessing an extraordinary mind and soul sensitivity, the great Simone Weil wrote the following, deeply reminiscent of the work of both Eigen and Bion, in *The Illiad*, or the *poem of force* (as quoted by Sheldon Bach, 1994, p. xv):

> To define force – it is that x that turns anybody who is subjected to it into a *thing*. Exercised to the limit, it turns man into a thing in the most literal sense: it makes a corpse out of him … Here we see force in its grossest and most summary form – the force that kills. How much more varied in its processes, how much more surprising in its effects is the other force, the force that does *not* kill, i.e., that does not kill just yet … From its first property (the ability to turn a human being into a thing by the simple method of killing him) flows another, quite prodigious too in its own way, the ability to turn a human being into a thing while he is still alive. He is alive; he has a soul; and yet, he is a thing. An extraordinary entity this, a thing that has a soul. And as for the soul, what an extraordinary house it finds itself in. Who can say what it costs it, moment by moment, to accommodate itself to this residence, how much writhing and bending, folding and pleating are required of it.

In Eigen's reading, Bion's psychoanalytic sensibilities and tireless work support a deep understanding of psychic deadness in reviewing various concepts such as (a) cultivating an attitude of "no-thing,"[6] (b) the impact of the *negative grid* in terms of functioning as a *catastrophe machine*, leading to forms of (c) *moral violence* if not psychic murder. For Eigen's Bion, the no-thing acts as a guardian against our propensity to concretize, literalize, and objectify the psyche. Mental life should remain immaterial and intangible. *Thingifying* the psyche needs to be slowed down, retarded by cultivating the attitude of the no-thing, "For Bion the tolerance of the no-thing is linked with modulated openness and learning from experience" (Eigen, 1996, p. 46). If the no-thing is eradicated, psychic murder may become evident; "Bion characterizes psychic murder as *moral* violence. The conviction that the object is no-thing itself can act as a coercive demand that the object be more and less than what is possible. The psyche becomes entangled in the reductionistic misuse of basic categories and functions, e.g., space, time, causality, and definition" (1996, p. 49). Eigen visually represents Bion's rich cogitations, wherein the internal and external object(s) are imbued with phantasy and imaginative potential (due to the fantasy pumps inherent in the psyche) able to facilitate psychological growth and/or entropy as follows (Eigen, 1996):

The symbol ˙ here is used to indicate the object or even where the object was, or is not. The symbol ↑ represents the undoing of meaning (internal saboteur) and ↓ states the opposite. The symbol ← represents the undoing of psychic work and even the use of various mental capacities as seen in disorders such as alexithymia, and → states its opposite. Including type A to C communication fields (Langs, 1976, 1977) the symbols ꝃ ꝅ communicate the constant and complex interaction between ↑,←,→, ↓ resulting in attitudes or artifacts (§ / Y/ ℞/ Δ/ ¥[7]) to be thought and experienced, or not. The symbols ← and ↑ are taken up in rich phenomenological discourse in *Psychic Deadness* (1996), *Toxic Nourishment* (1999), *Damaged Bonds* (2001a), *Feeling Matters* (2007), *Emotional Storm* (2005) and *The Birth of Experience* (2014a), to name a few. In the container-contained, *receptivity* welcomes psychic material and uses it for transformations. Even with trauma, primary process work may still support meaningful transformations; primary process impacts being transformed into useable images ↔ (into) symbols ↔ (into) thoughts. Unfortunately, overstraining the container, being *thingified*, or being subject to the many destructive variations[8] of the *negative grid* (Bion's *Catastrophe Machine,* in Eigen, 1998, p. 199), finds a psyche unable to flourish. Such a psyche may have been exposed to, if not continues to be exposed to, psychological transformations that grind bits of experience into nothingness. Most frightfully stated, malevolent precocity becomes a "force that continues after … it destroys existence, time and space" (Bion, in Eigen, 1998, p. 99). Subtler forms also exist and require Bion's *no-thing psychology*. Eigen writes that Bion continuously warns that a reductionistic misuse of the psyche and its effects, a form of intellectual hortus siccus, may serve as a basis for moral violence. *Moral violence* may contain violence to time and space, the overuse of causality, and restrictive definitions. To counter moral violence, Eigen's thinking on "I don't know" (2011) adds much relief; "perhaps we need to practice feeling and saying, 'I don't know,' like a musician practices scales, as part of an exercise in living" (2011, p. 80). "It's a grace to be able to finally say out loud, 'I don't know'" (2011, p. 82). "A certain kind of unknowing supports speech. *There is a taboo against not knowing in the culture*" (2011, p. 82; emphasis added). Within moral violence, experience cannot build, thinking-feeling rhythms may become foreclosed, concretizing attitudes may predominate (hypo-symbolization), and *causal-thinking only attitudes*

prevail (excessive calculative logic[9]). For Eigen, "Causal thinking readily lends itself to hardening of psychic arteries" (1996, p. 50). As such, thinking, or the *knowledge game* struggles to tolerate gaps, nuances, endless shifts, and the many corrections needed in day-to-day living. Thinking-feeling that enables to see, smell, hear, feel, digest, and work on emotional reality may remain underutilized. Cultivating a thinking-heart may soften defensive causal-like cognition, in time transcending rigid attentional styles. A more fruitful relationship may be cultivated between so-called differentiated and undifferentiated modes of mental functioning, i.e., rational thought and image-making,[10] enlivening thought-feeling dead spots and stagnation.

> Higher-level thinking may work overtime to cover defects in affective processing. The individual, for example, may use naming and definition to bind or contain persecutory feelings rather than explore them ... In such an instance, the individual has all he can do to keep up with his self-attacks or nameless dreads and imitations of catastrophe. He has all he can do to try to cauterize his sense of fragmentation or put a verbal tourniquet around disintegration. Here the aim of naming is to stop the horrible movement. *The result is the proliferation of elements meant to tie the psyche up rather than to enable it to evolve.*
>
> (1996, p. 54; emphasis added)

Protecting thoughts and feelings against *premature harvest* in the Bionian sense is also of importance. However, it should be evident that all types of thinking-feeling may be subject to a unique pulse or rhythm – a way of being-in-the-world. Bion's moral murder is a widespread killing of the psyche and the thinking heart itself. Effects of such a way of being-in-the-world can be found in Eigen's *deadening triad*, specifically, Eigen's *stupor-hallucinosis-megalomania* phenomena. Stupor-hallucinosis-megalomania are all attempts to undo meaning, ridding the self of the no-thing, a reflection of being subject to thingification, in turn, thingifying. That is, in stupor, one rids oneself of the no-thing, filling it with numbness, versus cultivating a state of creative emptiness. In hallucinosis, there is an evacuation of mental debris that could have stood for thinking. In megalomania, one does not find a transformative high, the high of "a godlike moment of revelation" (1996, p. 47), but of arrogance, a closing of learning from experience. A dead and deadening mind arrested in "a kind of narcotic electrocution" (Eigen, 1996, p. 48). These no-thing artifacts lead to a painful psychic register of countless adaptation and defenses. However, Eigen emphatically adds that primary process processing could "keep the clinical atmosphere open" (1996, p. 43). Being patient may allow thought-feelings to ripen. In psychoanalytic waiting and resting, regrouping can occur, and as such, the ability to process stupor-hallucinosis-megalomania thinking-feeling globs within primary process processing. Similar to the Haleakala silversword, certain meanings and thoughts live in a particular environment and flower once and die soon afterward, but not without scattering its drying seeds (Teitelbaum, 2020). Various trauma globs see the psyche unable to believe its thinking-feeling capacity, and experiences may turn persecutory too rapidly for the mind to respond, in turn stimulating a tragic sense of futility and depression. Building up and breaking apart (in creativity) rhythms are replaced by evacuation, mental shut down, magical thinking, and more. The psyche may even become cemented and cementing, foreclosing growth,[11] more painfully, cultivating a moralizing attitude, rigidly collapsing affective links between thoughts, serving as a kind of thinking-feeling superglue. Reflective of such attitudes remain the demand that *total and absolute control ought* to be possible and that any difficulty is *caused by something or someone*. Omnipotence and omniscience permeate such an affective atmosphere and forms of mentalization. It may also be evident, as mentioned by Bion, that omnipotence and omniscience serve as the impetus to forces that destroy existence, time, and space. Creatively and symbolically, I am reminded of the film *Ad Astra* (2019), wherein a father's megalomanic preoccupation nearly destroyed both his son and the earth. The father's loss of scientific meaning and emotional emptiness not only wiped out his own sensitive self and his love of his son, but almost all of humanity. A catastrophic tragedy – although frequently encountered in culture.

Eigen's vision: cultivating the capacity to serve as an auxiliary deep processor

We are indeed fortunate to find Eigen's psychoanalytic creativity deeply embedded in primary process work: "I must confess I am a primary process lover. In an important way, loving the flow of primary process meanings has made my life worthwhile" (1996, p. 142). Given the destructive forces evident in history, and as such, the intrapsychic and interpersonal stress each individual must accommodate and assimilate throughout his or her life, the work of Eigen brings much hope and faith in the psyche's ability to develop and find ways to stitch together a personality, especially after it has been exposed to too much or too little. Within the psychological areas discussed, *primary process work* as capacity is viewed as central in Eigen's approach to the psyche's deadness-aliveness dialectic (or scaling mount shock).

> Primary process work links personality together. One can use many images to express this linkage. It is the blood of personality, circulating throughout personality structures, issuing nutriments throughout the psychic body. It stimulates, warms, inspires, scares, and incessantly breaks apart and puts together experience in startling ways. When it works well, it facilitates the overall growth of personality.
>
> (1996, p. 143)

Similar to Bion's notion of the analyst serving as an auxiliary Other enabling alpha-functioning, so Eigen too holds that the analysand's *impact* should be welcomed, tolerated, held, and processed over time, as it reflects the primary raw datum in need of the analyst's faith, and utmost loyalty.

> [The] core ingredient ... is the impact of the patient on the therapist. *Impact is primary raw datum. It is the most private intimate fact of a meeting. The therapist may hide yet secretly nurse the deep impact the patient has on him.* To put the impact into words too soon may spoil its *unfolding.* An impact needs time to take *root and grow.* It occurs instantaneously, but needs the analyst's faith, time, and loyalty in order to prosper.
>
> (1996, p. 143; emphasis added)

Serving as one processor to another, Eigen forewarns that impacts require both *welcoming gestures* as well as periods of *incubation* (Eigen, 2020). Total, if not premature disclosure of another's impact may needlessly injure; that is, seeing too much of oneself too quickly and too fully may destroy the psyche's natural unfolding.

> But full disclosure of the impact may be destructive. One plays for time and protects and nurses the impact. In some instances, it may be years before an impact can be fully revealed, and by the time the patient has a different impact, although something of the original impact remains.
>
> (1996, p. 143)

In summary, it can be said that Eigen's psychoanalytic sensibilities as an "auxiliary deep processor," or an "auxiliary primary processor" allows for more than a classical defense analysis approach to psychic deadness. Rather, Eigen reminds the analyst to cultivate primary process attitudes able to lime psychoanalytic creativity so as to scaffold, cultivate, elucidate, and bridge lack in/of *psychological equipment;*[12] "Primary process begins the transformation of pain" (1996, p. 20). An analysand stated it as follows:

> Therapy here with you is necessary – it is my dialysis; without it, I am not sure I would make it through. There was too much trauma. I miss the very place the damage took place as I miss the moments that there was joy. There is no joy out there in the world, just adapting, surviving, no respite ... Here, I can process these toxins. I need to do this before I develop *emotional dementia.*

Eigen adds, as our deep *wisdom-processor*:

> On the other hand, primary process may never catch up to the sense of injury. Sensitivity to wounds may always be steps ahead of processing ability.

The growth in ability to live with this asymmetry is a kind of wisdom. One learns to give pain time. It gives time for pain to diminish enough for processing to begin nibbling at it. *The seasoned personality is steeped in time.*

(1996, p. 21)

Rising from the ashes – Eigen's Ferenczi

Psychic deadness brings into full view the various forces that severely challenge our sense of wholeness, vitality, and our *going-on-being-"with"*. It may undoubtedly be true that the damage for some is so comprehensive that *going-on-being-with* will remain a daily struggle. Eigen's poemagogic reading of Freud, Winnicott, Klein, Bion, and Ferenczi sees hopeful gestures in adapting to the evolutionary demand analysts face when working with the psychotic and dead-"ened" self. For Eigen, "I mention Ferenczi now because he stands as a beam of light, explicitly emphasizing the importance of the *analyst's love* in counteracting destructive forces" (1996, p. xix). For Sandor Ferenczi,[13] the dangers of a deadened psyche are real, especially when parents do not align themselves with the life force of their infant, "lest it slip into nonbeing to which it is so close" (Eigen, 1986, p. xix). To add to this lack of vital alignment the infant, and later child, may also be exposed to parenting practices that are experienced as intrusive and traumatic, serving as basis for traumatic imitation, the introjection of the guilt of the aggressor, traumatic progression, or precocious maturity (Eigen's *mind object*), excessive care-taking, and the emergence of the Orpha-fragment of the psyche, and more. Furthermore, the awareness of being subjected to an "alien will" (1995, p. 82)[14] can find the person in "a state of insecurity *resembling an earthquake*" (1995, p. 82). As such, an area of the personality may disintegrate into

a mass of atomized debris. The task of the analyst is to bring the psyche back to life out of these ashes. Day after day, first modest, then a progressive consolidation of the ashes into fragments of insight. At times everything will be destroyed again, then patiently built up again, until finally the experience of transference, and its implicit lesson in suffering, will smooth the path towards the traumatic depths.

(1995, p. 82)

Eigen's adds:

The spiral can reach a point where images of damage are fewer symbols than they are instances of the damage itself, momentary glimpses of the damaging process in progress. In extreme cases, the damage is so severe that images are no longer produced or are inaccessible, and the individual begins to vanish as the wounds close over him or her.

(1996, p. 22)

Despite such psychic difficulty, through Eigen's unique language, his creative psychoanalytic vision, and clinical touch, our own creative, still, and quiet center may grow anew through primary process work, as "Everything else revolves around it, grows out of it, guards it, extends it" (1996, p. 81).

Notes

1 According to Severn (1933/2017, p. 137): "To be sure, many people are 'dead' long before they pass out of this life; they become stultified and are incapable of living, even though they may go through the motions of doing so. A new vision is needed of the livingness of all experience, with a conception of life as a creative evolution."

2 Similar to the sun, Jupiter is composed predominantly of both hydrogen and helium, although, unlike the sun, it lacks the necessary amount to initiate *fusion (anti-union and defensive distinction dialectics)*, that is, the process that *fuels a star*. It also may have a solid core although given the gaseousness of the planet this is uncertain. Psychodynamically a rich metaphor!

3 See Eigen (1996, chapter 13), "Being too good."

4 See the case of Deborah, in Eigen (1996, pp. 17–18).

5 See "Disaster and horror: splitting and spinning" in Eigen (1995, pp. 158–160).

6 Also review Eigen's "I don't know," in 2011.

7

§ = fusion	Ꝏ/ = reversed fusion, fusion in reverse	Δ = oedipal situation	Y = one fused becomes two	¥ = highly differentiated me – you matrix (extreme opposite of "fused")
• = where object is or was	↓ = creation of meaning	↑ = undoing of meaning	→ = psychic work	← = undoing of psychic work
↳ ↑ ↲ ↩· →	Interaction between psychic work to create meaning and undoing of such work and meaning.			
t↓t				

8 See especially Eigen's use of "Grid thinking" given the impact of impacts in Eigen (2014, chapter 1, pp. 50–54).

9 See the work of Lesley Murdin (2021).

10 The work of Anton Ehrenzweig, *The Hidden Order of Art* (1967), explores the importance and interrelationship between differentiated and undifferentiated modes of mental functioning and calls for a "poemagogic" approach to psychic development.

11 Please see Eigen's summary of PS↔D2 Grid notation in Eigen (1996, p. 52).

12 Eigen mentions, "Deficit of equipment can be experienced as emptiness" (1996, p. 145).

13 Review Ferenczi's *Clinical Diary* (1995) entries of both 7 April 1932, "The fate of children of mentally ill parents," pp. 80–83, as well as of 12 April 1932, "The relaxation of the analyst," pp. 83–86. Eigen's thinking is very reminiscent of Ferenczi's clinical sensibilities and descriptions.

14 For Winnicott it is a moral sin, an unthinkable catastrophe to seep into the core of another and "steal him from himself" Eigen (1996, p. 81).

Chapter 6

In the beginning ... there was nourishment–trauma

> To some degree, processing detoxifies destructive affect. Unprocessed – unprocessable – destructive affect can become malignant ... the mother, to whatever degree possible, detoxifies the baby's destructive feelings and feeds back something more tolerable. Insofar as this fails, toxins build. Absence of detoxification capacity enables emotional life to poison itself.
>
> (Eigen, 2011, p. 47)

The annihilated self: annihilation with a thousand faces

In both *Toxic Nourishment* (1999) and *Damaged Bonds* (2001a), Eigen explores the myriad of subtle ways *coming into being with* remains subject to annihilatory and contamination processes. The fear of being overpowered, aggressively minimized, maimed, and murdered accompanies the *inviolable I* daily – from the cradle to the grave. Annihilatory and nulling realities dialectically and intimately shape psychic autopoiesis. Parents, educators, even politicians threaten, if not feed, our collective fear. End of world ("ing") phantasies abound and are known to most. The presence of an annihilated and ravaged self, being zombified and living as ghostliners, attests to its persistence. Supporting the therapeutic unfolding of a ruined self, its devastation as it "breaks into" another, and tolerating being annihilated together, are all central to Eigen's psychoanalytic ethic. Clinically, the annihilated self comes close to many works on the *baby in the drawer*, the stasis child-self, smothered and left devitalized by various development processes. Being and feeling alive may remain dangerous for many individuals,[1] given such development. For Eigen, all psychological life as known, despite our best intentions, consists of painfully laboring the facticity of our nourishment ∞ trauma experiences, a *nourishment–trauma dialectic* in need of a psyche capacity supporting the evolution of the *sensitive self* (2004). Eigen explores in volumes such as *Toxic Nourishment* (1999) and *Damaged Bonds* (2001a) how the sensitive self within

DOI: 10.4324/9781003002871-8

its *distinction–union structure* requires a *rhythm of faith experience* (Eigen, 1986, 1999, 2011) able to creatively work with parental care and love that reflect a mixed nourishment–trauma demand.

> Thus love is mixed with a variety of tendencies, including anxious control, worry, death dread, ambition, self-hate. Parental love is not pure ... The child must digest messianic expectations fused with everyday life. *To an extent, we learn to use what psychic nutriments we can and avoid what is toxic* ... In different measures, no one escapes toxic elements in nourishment secured.
>
> (1999, p. xv; emphasis added; emphasis)

Following in the footsteps of Elkin and others, Eigen's notion of the *sensitive self*[2] (Eigen, 2004), as found in works such as *Damaged Bonds* (Eigen, 2001a) and *Toxic Nourishment* (1999), finds the autochthonous s*elf* laboring under the strain of too much or too little parental love (even hate), necessitating desperate adaptations to ward off Winnicott's *primary agonies*, not to mention Bion's *nameless dread*. Eigen compassionately writes, similar to Winnicott, that development can go wrong as personality *starts to organize and come-into-being-with*, cultivating many toxic-nourishment fall-out scenarios to be contained in a *breakdown–recovery* pattern.

> Something goes wrong as personality begins to form, at the onset of self-organization, so that birth of self goes awry. One suffers distortion or is blown away. One tightens oneself to get through, but self-tightening creates distorted casings around distorted insides, hardening and poisoning self. One holds vast areas of self at a distance, but poison spreads and there is no safe haven. Winnicott speaks of *two kinds of persons*, one who does not carry around with them a significant experience of a mental break-down in earliest infancy and those who do. Those who do try to escape breakdown with one foot and move toward it with the other. *Therapy provides a place to embrace this double movement and develop a better rhythm so that the breakdown-recovery movement can be fruitful.*
>
> (2004, p. 23; emphasis added)

As previously written (Daws, 2021), Eigen argues that an infinite amount of psychosomatic variations and permutations exist in trauma-nourishment. The loss of goodness in, and of, the (M)Other's ministrations serves as the foundation to not only the loss of primordial consciousness (in need of *resurrection*, Ferenczi's psyche *ashes*), but also to the primordial awakening of the destructive malevolent Other ("fear nucleus," mount shock, Chapters 3 and 5), a destructive process only salvageable by the merciful Other's continuous ministrations. That is, our collective breakdown–recovery process is in need of a merciful Other to counter stupor, disaster anxieties, and the commencement of the psychotic self with its corrupted mind–body splits[3] (Eigen, 1986, 1996, 1999, 2001a). Eigen describes the loss of goodness as follows:

> Loss of goodness *mushrooms* [...] From pristine radiant awakening to mental-spiritual agony and death, loss of primordial consciousness, *a breaking of heart-to-heart, eye-to-eye, face-to-face contact.* Simple radiant identification of primordial self with primordial Other tastes destruction. In time the Other's *ministrations take hold, and primordial consciousness is reborn.* Or perhaps the infant experiences a spontaneous change of state, with correlative shifts of self-other feeling. *The overall movement is a kind of death-resurrection sequence.* However, with the rebirth of consciousness, the Other *acquires new significance. The self experiences regeneration in consequence of the Other's raising it from death.* Spirit has been *fanned back to life with awareness* of the Other as the eternal, numinous, Source of Being ...
>
> (2004, pp. 19–20; emphasis added)

> *Before the infant is aware of physical death, he has undergone many psychological deaths and rebirths.* By the time awareness of physicality as such arises, the experience of the loss and return of consciousness has been well established as a governing, underlying pattern. It remains as the unconscious background upon which future threats and dramas are played out ... The *rebirth archetype*[4] becomes the mold for further experience, no matter how bad things get, the unconscious can produce an image of a *saving other*[5] which protects one's integrity. If this is an illusion, it can be a salutary one.
>
> (1992, p. 22; emphasis added)

Registering and surviving, holding, and relating within *primary process impacts* as described in Chapter 5, analyst and analysand may come to see the unfolding of breakdown–recovery in various archetypal rhythms; birth–growth and damage–rebirth rhythms, trauma–nourishment rhythms, nourishment as trauma rhythms, integration ↔ disintegration rhythms (2001a, p. 153) and *healing longing in search of*, for Eigen, a *unique rhythm of faith.* The rhythm of faith touches those developmental moments where the self is exposed to death, entombment, and lack, calling forth the *resurrection principle* as described by Patrick Casement (2020), and so evident in the biography of Harry Guntrip (see Hazell, 1996). A deeply felt dream by Eigen's analysand Mac painfully illustrates the trauma–nourishment rhythms within family demands;

> Still a child, dressed in the little blue Navy suit modeled on the one my father wore, *I lie in a casket* in a dim room lighted only by candles. All

the family is there, hushed, seated in a circle, like mannequins frozen in formal poses and ritual gestures. I am calm (perhaps for the first time.) All struggle is gone, all protest. I accept what has happened in a spirit of love. Only one thing remains. A request. Without moving I ask them to make an exception to a rule that I already know cannot be broken. But it is the thing I need more than anything. And so I ask them again to bring Brownie, the teddy bear I love, and place him to me so I won't be alone. It is a plea but there is no panic in it, yet no hope that it will be heeded. And so finally in the great rush of what must be love I accept it all. It is what they've been waiting for, the thing that enables them to cry. The cry grows. It is the bond that unites them, giving them the identity they need to be a family. This knowledge is the central reality that frees me to what I now know I must do. I'm alone then, down in a crypt, in a cold stone place, a realm of shadow in a dim twilight. I go forward, toward a casket. I see myself lying there, in it – and I become what I see. A child is sleeping, beautiful and resigned. The beginnings of a smile are frozen on his lips. But no one will come to kiss them back to life. He will stay like this forever. He is sleeping but he will not awaken. ... *y hunch is that if we get to the annihilated self we will find a dead child. That dead child is, of course, oneself.*

(Eigen, 2006b, pp. 34–35)

A love, a phantasy bond that silences the sensitive self; a family bond of death, nourishing a dangerous yet beatific resignation – waiting for an enlivening kiss, the merciful Other, although

One has to die to keep the family together, a death that is part of socialization. A toxic bond, a damaged bond acting as personal and social cement. The dream expresses a dying out or mock death that goads Mac to speak. Keep the family together, no matter how impossible. Keep the self together, no matter how impossible. We are speaking of *existential nuclei, inner dead babies, or almost-dead babies*, or *pretend death*. This is a precious transmission. Love is an awful force to keep one down. Mac is telling us he refuses to be quiet. He will not go through his whole life watching the death of himself, a ghost of himself, a sleeping beauty akin to the mysterious resignation of Peter Pan's mother.

(Eigen, 2006b, p. 36; emphasis added)

Love, betrayal, guilt, and sacrifice play a pivotal role in all families, especially in traumatogenic families. Mac's exquisite sensitivity to the volarization of self in service of tribal unity and its impact on vitality and the annihilation of self remains breathtaking. Being oneself and coming alive can have detrimental effects on the maternal Other and family, not to mention one's tribe as found in sacralized violence and scapegoating. Even with false self adaptations, as with all of Eigen's writing (especially 1999, pp. 150–154), there remains a deep struggle to what is and feels alive in relation to the various forces working against such feeling. Progress itself, for many, can be traumatic – *progress as trauma*. Despite the latter, and similar to Eigen-in-the-crib listening to radio sound, the psyche will focus on whatever signs of life can support an *organizing experience*. Eigen tunes into nourishment–trauma, lack, and potential continuously, if not simultaneously; "Micro-shot after micro-shot, as if burrowing into micro-moments and letting them speak, sometimes a quivering kind of speaking, often part of a lifelong scream, sometimes joyous" (Eigen, 2020, p. 67). Eigen creates the awareness that the psyche naturally *reaches to what feels alive. The psyche also reaches from what may have felt dead and deadening, an aliveness–deadness archetype in service of activating a primordial, pre-conceptual, resurrection process.* Eigen's sensitive descriptions also find that nourishment and toxins are so interwoven that they are at times too difficult to differentiate, an essential reminder to contemporary clinicians under the sway of ever-increasing binary epistemologies:

> Emotional nourishment and poisons can be so interwoven that it is difficult, if not impossible, to tell the difference between them. The problem can be so extreme that nourishment one needs to support life is toxic, or worse, *one learns to extract what nourishment one can from poisons at hand.*
>
> (Eigen, 1999, p. xiii; emphasis added)

Analysands frequently have to make use of what they have been given and find solutions that support life further. Many have come to accept a limited and limiting goodness–badness balance, even comply. Some have given up specific ways of being in the world, attempting to remain at least connected and alive with the other. Others find partial solutions and areas of transformation while some live seemingly charmed lives, although dazed and diminished.

Reading Eigen, it becomes imperative to cultivate capacities able to *differentiate* emotional, interpersonal, and environmental (cultural, political) nourishment, i.e., nourishment that has a sense of goodness able to stand in creative tension to inevitable toxins, from those exposed to types of toxic nourishment that "wreak havoc" with our "psychobiological substrate" (see Alice, in Eigen, 1999, chapters 1, 4, 11), calling for different psychoanalytic holding and care. Similar to the work of Masterson and others, Eigen also describes, as a continuation of his psychic deadness theme of *being too good*, the link between suicide (psyche death) and lack of true self-support, irrespective of a so-called idyllic upbringing.[6] Narrow molds and pot-plant parenting find toxic nourishment contained in physical illness, suicide, miscarriage, and beyond, our "silent agonies" (p. xvi) with a thousand faces.

Fortunately, it is also evident in Eigen's psychoanalytic writing and technique that our silent agonies stand in creative relationship to "*the life no poison can kill*" (Eigen, 1999, p. iii). In Eigen's rhythm of faith, toxic nourishment brings forth our sustainment in "a *feeling of goodness with conviction*" (p. xvii), or in Bion's thinking, "*well-being and vitality springs from the same characteristics which give trouble*" (Bion, 1965, p. 144, in Eigen, 1999, p. xx; emphasis added). "Hope" in what gives trouble! Psychoanalytically, coming through the damage can bring an incredible sense of solidity, goodness, and vitality in relationship to self and others.

Despite such a reality, even possibility given the value of rebirth, dealing with toxic nourishment finds us preferring a bug-free universe (Eigen, 1999, chapter 4), cultivating dismissive styles that fail to support metabolizing the inherent toxins of being a sensitive self. Such dismissive attitudes become, in time, taken in as endo-psychic and interpersonal *self-nulling tendencies*. Eigen explores these *self-nulling tendencies* and realities creatively in his transformative three *Eigen in Seoul* volumes (2010, 2011, 2021), *Flames from the Unconscious* (2009), and *The Challenge of Being Human* (2018). An analysand, whom I will call Sarah, reflected on Eigen's damaged bonds as she discussed a rather neglectful childhood:

> I was always the caretaker, always. *It is me, the only me, or part of me?* It reminds me of pictures I saw when I was young of trees and people forgetting objects next to them. The trees eventually grow around the objects, engulf it. It becomes part of the growth rings of the tree, and damages the tree's growth rings. In time, trees can heal damage, this kind of damage from without, but it settles deeper in the tree with time ... You can see it in the tree's cross-sections, where there was damage. Frequently these foreign objects become permanently part of the tree and cannot be removed without damaging the tree forever, maybe even killing the tree. That is what I am feeling now – perhaps this history of mine cannot be removed without destroying me? I am not certain.

Sarah's toxic nourishment reflects damaged bonds, the bonding process *per se*, the forging of links as we hatch from our primordial being in the world to the realities of living with others. We are nurtured and damaged by the very bonds that supply life. Mutual impacts sustain as much as limit the I-Thou. Mutuality becomes structural – a structural osmotic nourishment–trauma interplay. As described in Chapter 5, the psyche is exposed to damaged and damaging bonds, although the psyche continually attempts to work its impacts (primary process work as an *epicormic* drive?). As an analytic reader, one can think of works such as Jeremy Hazell's (1996) psychoanalytic biography of Harry Guntrip, Linda Hopkin's book *The False Self: The Life of Masud Khan* (2006), Marion Milner's masterpiece *The Hands of the Living God* (1969/2010), and Marie Cardinal's *The Words to Say it* (1983), to name a few. Reading such work, one meets Eigen's notion that *damaged bonds and damaged dream-work function together.* "Many dreams are concerned with trying to process wounds to our psychic digestive system. Wounded dreamwork tries to cure itself. It tries to heal or depict its injured state. It tries to get at the damaged bonds that warp, block, or immobilize its efforts" (Eigen, 2001a, p. 5).

Building further on Bion's notion of the *murderous superego* (Kafka's torture machine – the Harrow apparatus[7]), Eigen accentuates the various struggles to dream a damaging object that no amount of dream-work can put together again. A struggle that both inhibits and devastates even unconscious processing. Through Eigen's various case studies, the reader finds the kind of psychoanalytic hope so poignantly written on by Guntrip (Hazell, 1996, pp. 302–303), i.e., that the work of analysis may help clear "rubbish," meeting lost parts of the self, "mentally stocking up" against what remains to be resurrected and rebirthed. Eigen's work holds the hope that in dreaming the analysand may be protected from catastrophic aloneness (Father, why have thou forsaken me?) and against the damaged, threatening, or damaging *self and object* in the unconscious. Eigen's session with Andrè Green comes to mind as well as Alice's dream (1999):

Alice's dream: A doctor removed what seemed like an infinity of micro tongue depressors from Alice's mouth. Like the sorcerer's apprentice, the more he took out, the more they multiplied. He persisted, finally, they began to dimmish.

(1999, p. 7)

Eigen on Alice's dream: We took this as an image of depression from an early age. The nipple was depressing instead of nourishing: perhaps depression was the nourishment. I pictured Alice's mouth filled with particles of glass, not simply tongue depressors. What dreadful inhibitions she had to fight in order to function! Oral rape. A splintered mother stuffing her psychotic fragments into her daughter. Quite a feed! To use herself at all (to move her tongue, to taste life, to speak, to express feelings, to think, to be), Alice had to oppose an enormous destructive undertow.

(1999, p. 7)

Despite various creative possibilities evident in Eigen's clinical touch to wounded and wounding nourishment, Eigen also conveys a further astounding developmental complexity of breakdown in dream-work in discussing Bion's notion of *anti-synthesis tendencies* within the self. That is, given damaged nourishment, there may be a deep psyche need to *prevent the synthesis* of the *frightening superego* (in Klein's depressive position)! Eigen articulates it as follows (2001a, pp. 24–28 for greater detail):

(a) Similar to the work on the psychotic self (Eigen, 1986), the deadened self (Eigen, 1996), as well as Shelgold's *Soul Murder* (1999), the personality may have to contend with a most sudden kind of mind/T-ego and body-ego fright. The sudden fright (terror, shock, panic) may also, unthinkably so, be subject to repetition. The person born into a frightened or frightening world is primarily subject to a developmental context characterized by the absence of alpha functioning and subject to the *Omega function* (Williams, 1999; Daws, 2006). For Williams (1999), the *Omega function* derives mainly from the introjection of an object that is both impervious and overflowing with projections and can be found in disorganized, disoriented types of attachment. In such attachment, children have been exposed to parents who had themselves suffered trauma, and as such, are either frightened or frightening (or both; see Williams, 1999, pp. 246–247).

(b) Exposed to a fright or *Omega nucleus*, the personality may either collapse or congeal around the trauma (as in Sarah's tree and Saturn's moons). Considering Eigen's vacuum-evacuation diagram in *Toxic Nourishment* (1999, pp. 139–158), one can imagine the nucleus feeding the personality toxic elements, cancerously changing the personalities' DNA and RNA, warping *body-ego* and *T-ego* adaptations. The fear nucleus, to use spatial logic, may also expose the psyche to a "black hole" reality, sucking/robbing the vitality of the personality, leaving the psyche denuded of much-needed psychic building materials. Although less dramatic, the psyche may also be subject to psychopathic (dismissive attachments)-masochistic-psychosomatic transformations as explored in the work of Elkin (1958, 1972) and Eigen's *Psychic Deadness* (1996), which is similar to a "white-hole". Nothing can enter a white-hole's event horizon, and is subject to dispersal. T-ego and body-ego disconnect and antagonism (black-hole ⇌ white-hole) may prevail.

(c) Once the collapse has occurred, undoing remains notoriously challenging. Fortunately, most forms of collapse tend to be partial and the total collapse of a psyche rare. Although rare, one may be confronted with a type of *T-ego or body-ego catatonia,* and Eigen, similar to Harry Stack Sullivan, reminds clinicians that energy does remain in *being* catatonic and is frequently linked to pre-verbal postures (related to both biological and interpersonal proto-patterns). Collapse and breakdown are day- and night-time realities; wakemares and nightmares expressed by Eigen[8] as follows: "Still, there is more chronic broken-down-ness or areas of breakdown, which never seem to heal, which simmer and seep in insidiously stifling ways." (Eigen, 2001a, p. 24). Interventions in the distinction–union structure may make life possible or tolerable once again (1986, pp. 306–312).

(d) For Eigen's Bion, emotional truth can be a "frightful friend," similar to biblical prophets exposed to visual-physical (T-ego, body-ego) devastation by witnessing and experiencing truth; truth able to flood the body and mind. Realities may haunt and destroy, too difficult to endure and process. Living a lie, semi- or half-truths may be both temporary or permanent solutions preventing further catastrophe. Sue, hospitalized for a brief psychotic episode (T-ego shock), mentions to me: "My husband was a man of God (a theologian), but turned out to be the true incarnation of the devil. He stole funds and seduced women. What devastated me was not just his unimaginable acts, but *what* he said when I confronted him, 'You didnt know?' mocking my not-knowing, my farm girl mentality. It hit me, drove me into hospital – how could I not see it? How can I ever trust my gut and senses again?" Finally, from another sensitive analysand (body-ego shock), "When my father died, I suddenly struggled to see the letters on the blackboard, and when my husband left me many years later, I developed cataracts at 40!"

(e) Fright, given its psycho-physical-spiritual impact, *infinitizes* and gives birth to "an intractable Idea of Fright" (Eigen, 2001a, p. 24). Similar to the Old Testament God, if not the various destructive figures in mythology, frightening parental impact may warp the personality seeing it "stifled by this terror. Abrupt, alarming moments become an Eternal Idea, Eternal Reality, although the face on everyone's fright is different" (Eigen, 2001a, p. 25). Becoming "stuck" in the Idea of Fright brings further fear as growing and moving forward implies gaps, unknown areas between the paranoid-schizoid and the depressive position. Similar to Fairbairn (1952) and Masterson (1972), a damaged self may become addicted or attached to the *bad object*. Leaving implies further dreads, as many feel ill-equipped for an Odyssey. Masterson articulated it as the deep abandonment depression, a loss of the good self and object that lies like a cyst submerged, coming to disruptive life in the activation of the so-called disorder of self triad: self-activation, feeling oneself, or connecting leads to anxiety and panic, which leads to defense. Better the devil, *you* know?

(f) Bion's superego as an organ of morality, becomes the destroyer of self (an epistemic Munchausen by proxy). The ego-destructive superego is not a typical morality but a tyrannical, if not monomaniacal assertion of superiority and specialness (intolerant object⁀ terrifying superego) (Eigen, 2001a, p. 40). The "self-destructive superego" (2001a, p. 25), according to Eigen, is both steeped in, and powered by, a formless dread, congealed into hate. Hate's influence draws on boundless dread. For

Eigen, hate and rage are thus ominously fed by dread and terror, in turn nurturing megalomanic and anti-life adaptations as described by Elkin.

(g) Eigen forewarns, given the impacts described and forces to be faced, *analytic nibbling* may serve the analytic enterprise better (1993, 1996, 1999, 2001a, 2004, 2005). However, there is a tendency to bite off too much, swallow, and be swallowed by experience.

Putting this together, for dreaming, the very object that destroys a thinking-feeling-psyche is to put together the very anti-dream object. Working and dreaming from the ruins of the anti-dream and the unspeakable object remains a profound challenge for the analyst as a participant. Rise in any emotions means shutting down, going under. Eigen mentions our cultural reminders of objects too good/bad (Medusa/God) that may not be touched/seen as the very act swamps and threatens to destroy the person. In Eigen's own descriptions:

> The object that cannot be dreamt, the anti-dream object, is often an amalgam of damaged/damaging primary objects (actions and aspects of mother / father / caretaker / milieu) fused with mutilated parts of the personality, which agglutinate / disperse / compress and undergo deformed magnification and rigidification.
>
> (2001a, p. 39)

> We [therapists] enable people to dream the undreamable and draw growth, stopping damage into dream-work that connects one with oneself. Dream-work is steeped in infinite heartbreak and terror, but there are, too, infinities of beauty that break the heart, like bread, in joy, which dream-work tastes, chews, digests, celebrates, crumb by crumb.
>
> (2001a, p. 61)

> It may be that a patient needs to be dreamt by an analyst before the former can make use of dreaming. He may need an experience of becoming a useful part of another's dream-work before getting the feel of using his own ... actually feel the other's alpha functioning working on him – mother bird pre-digesting him, ready to feed him to himself ... The analyst, at such moments, may be a kind of auxiliary alpha function or primary processor or dream-worker.
>
> (2001a, p. 65)

Relying on Bion's *alpha-function and dreamwork alpha*, Winnicott's transitional relatedness, as well as Eigen's own concept of the Other as an "auxiliary primary processor" in the area of *distinction–union* with "*on-off alpha*"[9] (2011, p. 67), toxic nourishment and damaged bonding experiences may be cultivated anew, finding an "infusion of life, spirit, feeling"[10](2011, p. 92). Although a seemingly romantic epistemology (also Eigen, 2001a, pp. 46–48), Eigen's *on-off alpha*, in tandem with Elkin, Bion, and Winnicott, creatively supports an attitude of no-thing and no-blame, protecting the embryonic psyche from further splitting and splintering in the *distinction–union structure*.

> A source of pain involves clinging to one or the other of dual states, exacerbating a conflict between embedded-emergent. On distinction-union planes, this translated to conflict between union-distinction tendencies. The situation is compounded when personality is subjected to catastrophic impacts which affect these tendencies as well as other capacities ... One thing that can happen is that the dual tendencies split off from each other, or try to, as each side or tendency thinks the other is causing the disturbance and that by somehow tearing at or trying to wipe out or dissociate from the other the disturbance will be solved. Distinction imagines if it gets rid of union, disturbance will disappear, and vice versa. In response to difficulty, capacities may reach breaking points and repudiate or overlay each other. Co-dependent capacities may struggle not to be co-dependent, as if either tendency could have existed independently of the other.
>
> (2011, pp. 14–15)

It is undoubtedly evident that many types and variations of *toxic nourishment fall-out*[11] exist and can be creatively explored in Eigen's *Psychic Deadness* (1996), *Toxic Nourishment* (1999), *Damaged Bonds* (2001a), *The Sensitive Self* (2004), *Emotional Storm* (2005), and *Feeling Matters* (2007) under headings such as being exposed to killers in dreams (2001a, 2005), moral violence (1996/ 2004), being too good (1996/2004), experiencing an annihilated self (2006b, 2007), suffering trauma clots (2007), experiencing empty and violent nourishment (1999), self-nulling tendencies (1999), experiencing the shadows of agony X (1999, broken X), fearing madness (1999), and suffering the undreamable object (2001a). All are meaningful signifiers to our psychotic, disorders of the self, and neurosis registers. Despite our damaged bonds and toxic nourishment registers, Eigen's notion of the ever-healing wound (psyche *wu wei*, Eigen, 2020), psychoanalytic faith, rhythm of faith, and faith's breath all provide much-needed *seelsorge* and solace. Eigen's psychoanalytic attitude and presencing ensure an archetypal "coming alive" in an *area of faith* deeply honoring our nourishment–trauma dilemma as well as our divine spark. In conclusion for Eigen:

> My sense is that over time nourishing aspects of the environment do get through (often osmotically): (1) if one does not totally succumb to the gravitational pull of damaging-object/damaged capacity; (2) if real

nourishing aspects outlast or co-exist with damaging aspects. Insofar as the possibility of nourishment is there, the possibility of someone noticing it may increase. Partly, it is a matter of mutual endurance, long-term interpenetration of nourishing/anti-nourishing forces, gradual shifts of balance.

(2001a, p. 70)

Notes

1 See also the work of Sabina Spielrein.
2 One cannot but marvel at the creative overlap between Eigen, Elkin, and the three areas of the mind as described by Michael Balint.
3 See Eigen's *psychotic self* concept, chapter 8, in *The Psychotic Core* (1986).
4 See Eigen's discussion in *The Psychotic Core* on Berdyaev's neontic freedom and Winnicott's formlessness, unintegration, madness, and suicide (1986, pp. 336–340).
5 Patrick Casement's *Credo* (2020, chapter 5) discusses "*the resurrection principle*" in Christianity and may be read here with both Elkin's and Eigen's deep concerns and sensitivities.
6 The Case of Doris, pp. xv, xvi, 18–34, 68, 75 in Eigen, 1999.
7 Kafka's torture machine called the Harrow apparatus/machine inscribed "Honor thy Superiors" on the back of prisoners (see *In the Penal Colony*).
8 Also see the work of Richard B. Ulman and Doris Brothers (1988), *The Shattered Self: A Psychoanalytic Study of Trauma* for descriptions and dreams similar to Eigen's observations.
9 For a detailed exposition on Eigen's *on-off alpha* as it relates to Bion see Eigen (2011, pp. 57–72).
10 As articulated by an analysand of Dr. Eigen called Kirk (2011, p. 92).
11 Also see the works of Paul Williams: *The Fifth Element* (2010) as well as *Scum* (2013).

Chapter 7

Eigen's radiant affective triptych

Emotional storms in ecstasy, rage, and lust

> Emotion is a double threat. Insofar as emotions represent life, it threatens the murderous superego, which is set in an anti-life mode.
>
> (Eigen, 2005, p. 143)

Eigen's psychoanalytic heartbeat

Eigen's affective triptych, its creation as a "response to an inner pressure to express the ecstasy [rage, lust, emotions] underlying psychoanalytic work" (Eigen, 2001b, p. vii), finds expression in "the psychoanalytic heart beating through a range of experiences significant for who we are; pleasures and pains – threatening to sink the soul – culminate in faith and openness" (2001, p. vii). Steeped in the creative work of various spiritual and religious wisdom traditions, Federn's *originary boundless I-feeling*, Winnicott's *going-on-being*, Milner's *orgasmic core of symbolic experiencing*, Bion's *Faith*, and Lacan's boundless *jouissance* (Eigen, 1993,[1] 1998), Eigen explores creative and destructive ecstasy, lust, and rage in three breathtaking essays (2001, 2002, 2006b). For Eigen, there can be ecstasy in anger, in rage, in destruction. Body ecstasies meet transcendental ecstasies, intermingle, following incessant amalgams only inhibited by our collective and personal imagination:

> Fear-rage ecstasies, erotic ecstasies, intellectual ecstasies (think Hanna Arendt on writing), power ecstasies, hate ecstasies, love ecstasies … Hitler ecstasies. Saint Teresa's ecstasies. Incessant amalgams of selfless-surrender, twin ecstatic poles. Sensation, feeling, thinking, intuition, willing, imagining, believing, disbelieving, knowing, unknowing, *all ecstasy vehicles*.
>
> (2001b, p. 29; emphasis added)

Eigen's Freudian touch accentuates the double movement between the I that appropriates and the I that consolidates the *desired* territory. For Freudian Eigen, the "*psychic magnifier-infinitizer* translates good to heavenly" (2001b,

DOI: 10.4324/9781003002871-9

p. 5), allowing a desert soul to see an oasis (an emotional Fata Morgana?).[2] The hungry baby hallucinates the breast; the human maximizes the pleasurable and good and obliterates the bad. The Freudian child remains caught in a perennial psychic conundrum, i.e., how to develop anti-hallucinatory capacities to allow painful reality, and in the process, simultaneously make room for ecstasy in relation to pain and loss? Eigen further mentions that, for both Elkin and Federn, the primordial I is not originally a *Freudian psyche* (a *magnifier-infinitizer*) but a "*child of God.*" A primordial I touching eternal, boundless, bliss meets body-ego hunger and pain that is instantaneously, miraculously, ecstatically, and blissfully transcended through the tender ministrations of the Other. Freudian superego will follow, becoming too quickly the damning anti-bliss ecstasy superego as described by Eigen (2001b, 2002), Grotstein (1981, 2007), and Chrzanowski (1973). Despite the dawn, if not possible eclipse of the superego over ego and id, it is the original "*Cosmic I*" (Eigen, 2001b, p. 7) as a primordial reality that will meet the Other as, and in, the Real. Eigen mentions emphatically, "One is not surprised to learn that primal, ecstatic, boundless I is on a collision course with the fact of life" (2001b, p. 7).

So many permutations are possible, from autistic retreats to the hardening of the T-ego and body-ego as a shell[3] (Reich's character armor, Eigen's *mind-object*). In contrast, lack of insulation finds "no-shell" and hallucinatory ecstasy, psychotic rapture, and blissful oceanic oneness detrimental to psychic anchoring (Eigen, 1986, on Schreber). *Oceanic feel ∞ claustrum adaptations* in a creative or destructive dialectic. Our good, "whole," and wholesome *I-feel* is certainly nourished by the continual I–Other dialectic, although the "I" indeed can, if not initially, hallucinate pleasure and fullness despite the Other. *Our primordial protective hallucinatory ecstasy-pain equipment is a psychological necessity.* Powerfully fragile, a fragile power. With time and the growing ever-present sense of transitional space between the I and the not-me, the knowledge *and* joy of the Other may indeed flourish. Although our I-feel may initially encompass the Other, if not the Other as feel, the Other as "not me" may come to complete and fulfill, cover lack and pain, and bring ecstasy as wholly Other; "You are *It* for me" (Eigen, 2001b, p. 8; emphasis added). Visual ecstasy (T-ego), vision-mind-distance ecstasy, mouth-nipple-inside-body ecstasy (body-ego), boundless I-feel, if not Eigen's "I- radiance" (2001b, p. 8) meets "You-radiance," and can be summarized as follows:

> *I-radiance, You-radiance: competing-complementary radiances.*
> *I-ecstasies, You-ecstasies: rings or ripples within-outside each other.*
> (Eigen, 2001b, p. 8)

Oceanic feel ∞ claustrum pulsations, and as such, *hellish ecstasy ∞ ecstatic hells* are all part of the distinction–union dialectic's mind-body ecstasy and torment, both permeating and complementing self and Other relatedness.

Eigen maps various "agony-ecstasy struggles evident in our original I-feel (original sin, pride, gluttony, etc.), mind-I-feel (omniscience, omnipotence, arrogance), body sense and feel (physical limitations, tiredness, disease, illness), predatory systems (Institutions), and the *Something More* (as principle)" (2001, pp. 22–24) that may come through as we survive moments of ecstasy-torment.[4] Similar to the biblical story of Bathsheba (lust, destruction, the birth of a son of wisdom), "something more" may come to hold fast, slowly grow, balancing, thickening, and enriching the dialectic between ecstasy-agony and agony-ecstasy. "I feel"–"You" gaps and losses become the following possibilities too:

> *I-agony, You-agony: competing-complementary radiances.*
> *I-agony, You-ecstasies: competing-complementary radiances.*
> *I-ecstasy, You-agony: competing-complementary radiances.*

Eigen furnishes these complex moments of joy-agony, ecstasy, and lust in describing Homer's *The Iliad* and the biblical story of Dinah. Wisdom literature serves as a psychoanalytic turning point where élan and curiosity, the play of sameness and difference, if not our erotic nuclei (2006b, p. 7) in perpetual Oedipal strife, meet the Freudian themes of violence, tribalism, violation, fertilization, and assimilation (Eigen, 2006b, pp. 7–20). For Eigen, similar to his creative analysand, aptly named *Sparrow* (2006b, pp. 38–46), we learn by bursts of joy, ecstasy, and lust. We grow and get injured by our passions, our desires, our lust-ecstasy-agony dialectic, hopefully, aided by and serving a growing rhythm of faith.

> "I am lusting my life away," she complained. "Following my bliss, my good feeling. Like crumbs in the forest, men, classes, jobs. Where are these crumbs leading me? My life eats at them and they're gone. Something remains, yes, but is anything building? I once thought they were diamonds, gems of experience. Now I want more, something else."
>
> (2006b, p. 45)

Ecstasy and aliveness, our lust for life, also evokes another theme close to Eigen's psychoanalytic heartbeat: *loss and mourning*, not only of self-experiences but also the needed Other. Losing another, in reality, or phantasy, finds agonizing adjustments to life. From the most primordial +Z dimension and its vertices, from loss of primordial consciousness to selfhood and abandonment depression, to neurotic melancholic adjustment, psychoanalysis has been a faithful servant and guardian. Eigen mentions, and rightfully so, that loss may also contain the warm glow of remembrance; that is, warm joyful memory floods experienced as a form of psychic milk able to nurture and lift loss and grief: grief and the grieving mind-heart-body as mouth meets the nourishing glow of the memory nipple[5] sustaining a rhythm of faith. In a beautiful work, *The Soul in Agony* (Corbett, 2015), the author gives the following example of Eigen's *loss-agony-glow*:

> And so suddenly, in that instance of full stop, I felt a swelling of energy emerge and expand in the centre of my chest. I felt like I was being opened up from the inside out. This was not a traumatizing experience in the least; rather it was like deep currents of energy were passing throughout my body and it felt incredibly refreshing. I was clear and alertly aware. As I accepted the entirety of my experience in the moment without any desire for escape I experienced a thinning away of my usual sense of self and replaced by a vast spaciousness that I had never before experienced before. I was truly stunned. *I realized that the essence of my pain was fed through my desire to be rid of it.* Strangely, my search for healing was an underhanded way of perpetuating its existence.
>
> (Brian Theriault, 2012, in Corbett, 2015, p. 220)

Eigen adds that where there is agony-ecstasy flow, there may also be agony-ecstasy clots, finding the possible development of emotional thrombosis in need of psychological anticoagulants. We need to develop the ability to work with both ecstasy and agony clots, our inherent human stuckness to simplify and choose one area over another, even setting limits on both one's ecstasy if not agony to "feel into" the other so as to experience the Other's difficulties in ecstasy-agony rhythms without superego collapse or violence. Failure and aborted attempts are beautifully articulated not only in Eigen's trilogy but can also be read in Sheldon Bach's *The Language of Perversion and the Language of Love* (1994). Can ecstasy be too much? That is, could "falling up" in ecstasy, experiencing new heights of creative and joyful achievement in self-feel, relationships, and work also lead to loss and agony? Ascension also has much to teach in a world that functions monoocularly – described by Eigen as "*The Jim Henson Complex*" (2001b, p. 58); that is, those that experience fame after extreme difficulty may also suffer dire psychological consequences.[6] A young pianist finds professional success and a satisfactory sexual experience only to be confronted with a diagnosis of cancer, or various creative men who find "new" enlivening relationships drown seemingly by accident. *Even positive changes call for the development of T-ego and body-ego capacities able to tolerate the difference.* Eigen writes:

> Henson got sick but ignored it, cough, chest congestion. By the time he sought medical help, he was in the process of drowning in his own lungs. He did not recover. My imaginal story: he became so successful that the space of his life grew so big that he could no longer feel himself fully. Self-feeling thinned lacking sufficient compression as life space became bigger

and bigger. Lungs filling up physically dramatized a need to fill space that could be filled. Not having a space small enough to feel yourself got acted out somatically.

(2020, p. 47)

Seeing both God and Medusa has consequences – being transfixed on either has effects, blinding and petrifying. Certain ecstasies, as personified biblically in Sodom and Gomorrah,[7] bring forth different limits. Looking back with longing, pining for lost ecstasies may have dire consequences. Fortunately, as the toponymic considerations teach us, there is an importance, a growing ability to move between being submerged in ecstasy-agony and fortifying and strengthening oneself – *coming up and coming through* in creative ways in Eigen's language of being. Many of man's most cherished biblical and philosophical teachings, and psychoanalysis remains but a single approach in a sea of possibility, attempt to dialogue on our ecstasy-agony tensions. Ecstasy may in time become increasingly agonizing (as in pining, Fairbairn's desirable-deserter), an agonized-self may be contorted into an ecstatic facsimile as compromise formation, as a defense, if not a desperate attempt at limited (Quixotic?) freedom; "When I feel I am falling away, when I am swamped by others, by life, to cut and bleed I sense a relief, a freedom, I feel alive … I am alive. Pain-alive ecstasy." However, if one holds religious text in context, many experiences are followed by other genres, texts that allow for continual ecstasy-agony work. Psychic buoyancy may be called upon not to get submerged for too long (and submersion is in itself of importance). Also, falling prey to "too much," i.e., too much structure and rules "against" our need to experience submersion[8] fails to take our sensuous, ecstatic, and lustful experiences into developmental account (Eigen, 2001b). Maternal–paternal balance in Eigen's and Elkin's way of holding a psychic dialectic remains essential.

Finally, we may protect children and adults by instructing them to "look away" from ecstasy-lust. In Eigen's psychoanalytic faith, coming through that which submerges, even if powerful in its capacity to petrify, may serve the psyche in developing the capacity needed to make use of our most primordial affects. Again I am reminded of J. K. Rowling's genius in her book volume *Harry Potter and the Prisoner of Azkaban*. In this installment, the children must learn a spell (saying aloud *Expecto Patronum*) that reflects each child's essential "good memory" to protect them against evil, such as the Dementors, or He-Who-Shall-Not-Be-Named. To practice, the children have to expose themselves by facing the very thing that scares them in confronting a mortal non-being called a Boggart, a shapeshifter. A stunning description – bogg[art], the art of being in the bog (Gomorrah), being bogged down. Being exposed to the emotional storm that constitutes our ecstasy-lust-rage nature is not pathology but part of our embryonic capacities in need of growth.

Emotional storm and feeling matters

Joy and ecstasy storms, grief storms, guilt storms, rage storms – implosion, explosion, all part of the emotional reality when two personalities meet. Coming-into-being finds the infant experiencing and involved in storms that are seemingly total, from bliss to utter pain (see Chapter 3). Bliss-pain as the foundation to our perennial death–resurrection rhythms, falling apart and coming together rhythms, building the necessary equipment needed to survive, sustain, and creatively work with various Eigensesque vertices such as omnipotence, omniscience, and mindlessness. Within these nuclear rhythms, new transformation and languages of achievement are forged, and breakdown–recovery sees birth–rebirth "with a thousand faces, although most of the time it is an aborted, even deformed, psychic birth" (2005, p. 10). We are all a once in a lifetime occurrence of coming alive↔ dying, trauma↔ recovery, repair↔ recovery↔ reconciliation, *breakdown↔ coming together*, and burial ↔ resurrection (Eigen, 2002, p. 89). Lopsidedly endowed, as Eigen often notes, our physical maturity out-paces our ability to *process feelings and inner reality, especially in breakdown*. Even the most basic emotions, such as grief, anger, fear, joy, etc., seem difficult to tolerate and be allowed their growth rhythms. Emotions are frequently (especially rage, lust, and ecstasy) *subject to being willed, falling under the domain of willful control, or blamed as bad will or lack of will*. Our primordial expressions and signifiers are unfortunately subjected to the realm of something to be *forgiven for*, rather than *for*-giving, *a given* of our sensitive self in emotional storms! If not *for-giving* we suffer a most insidious *rage-ecstasy-lust anomie,* if not *rage-ecstasy-lust ennui.* Emotional storms may enliven this human given, and ask, as Eigen does, for time and space; "Emotional storm is not pathology. It is part of reactivity, permeability, responsiveness – part of what happens when people meet. We are not sick because we are sensitive or sensitive because we are sick, unless we want to view human sensitivity itself as a kind of dis-ease" (2005, p. 19)

Eigen mentions that we live in a culture that normalizes a sort of insensitivity, a culture that cloisters emergent affective sensitivity, emotionally stigmatizing others as a way to rid the self of our most primal affective language. Do we not frequently hear, if not say, "you are too sensitive?" Mother and child, father and child, family and culture under the sway of constricting regulation and control ideologies, similar to the overuse of medication,[9] blocking our ability to work with our emotional nature. Sensitivity and primary storms in need of time, space, and recognition, rather than soundproofing or sanitizing adaptations. Eigen emphasizes *recognizing the Other, not just interpreting the Other*, which could serve as the basis for premature foreclosure. Winnicottian interpretation may be closer to Eigen's openness – that is, interpretation as showing another the limits of understanding. Daseinsanalysts hold interpretation as a form of *confession* to another. To protect from soul murder, we need to return again and again to the point of *mutual impact* as a way to sustain what is most precious in being human – our emotional sensitivity:

> Therapy provides an arena to experiment with aliveness-deadness. Still, therapy is real. If something goes wrong, a life can be destroyed. We hope therapy is a self-correctable process ... At any moment, a therapist may be too alive or dead for a given patient – at a given time, at a given way. And vice-versa. Therapist-patient are separate persons but also part of a larger emotional field made up of many regions and kinds of aliveness-deadness sensing each other, feeling each other out. One learns to tone X down, tone Y up, so that more nuances of communication become possible.
>
> (2001b, p. 49)

> I don't think feelings are getting digested today. There are massive social pressures to thin out or eject them like missiles at or into others (other groups, individuals, parts of self) ... *It often seems that on the individual level and for the body politic there's no emotional digestive system at all right now* ... Widespread emotional indigestion, psychic bellyaches (let alone heart-aches), moulded by calculation, manipulations, schemes, that try to order internal disorder ... *What we need now more than anything is a worldwide working emotional digestive system.*
>
> (2016, pp. 132–133; emphasis added)

Clinical Eigen, on his own impact on others, states:

> [Reflecting with an analysand George] I agree with George, feeling there is more that can be done. At the same time, I feel my warp, my twist. Congealed hate and fear, trauma corpses that never let go, a sickly tail one drags through the center of one's being. What have I done with it? Has it lessened over the years or come to take less space? It keeps burrowing like a spore deeper into healthy tissue,[10] into depths one didn't know existed. Yet I feel something has happened and keeps happening. Something does make a difference.
>
> (2002, p. 52)

> It remained to be seen to what extent I was capturing a bit of Warren's soul with my mind, smearing him with my own soul colors and mental categories, or opening myself to an impact that might pay off for him.
>
> (2002, p. 91)

To return to the therapeutic echo-chamber, it is evident that transformative contact between two subjectivities may frequently be interrupted by emotional storms. Emotional storm interruptions are to be found between mother and child, child and the world, within parts of the self, and reflect various mind–body adaptations. Emotional storms are, in essence, both mental-spiritual and somatic, i.e., mental-spiritual storms that meet body-storms in need of a "physical-emotive digestive system" (2005, p. 81). Clinically, Eigen discusses an analysand named Stacey who experienced a mind–body split akin to globus-hystericus. Being with Eigen, Stacey relates the complex interplay of her wished-for loving inner mother as shamed by the real external mother, Winnicott's subjective and objective mother at odds, creating a sudden spasm and recoil:

STACEY: Its back (pointing to her throat-chest area).
EIGEN: Your mother is stuck in your food pipe ... she is indigestible.
         (2005, p. 83; a non-ecstasy oesophageal bolus – a mental digestive clot)

Eigen mentions the instantaneous response, a product of their closeness. Silence ensues. Stacey repeats "indigestible," a meaningful mantra, taking in, tasting, liming her psychic digestive tract. In contrast to such liming, Eigen mentions chronic emotional colds, emotional lungs filled with psyche-spiritual mucous, undiagnosed emotional pneumonia, emotional black lung, and upheaval of mind-spirit-body (1986, 2001a, 2005). An analysand stated it as follows: "My smoke-filled marijuana existence that blotted out reality, my loss, my damage, I could not breathe, emotionally holding my breath." Eigen reminds the reader, reminiscent of the great Maurice Merleau-Ponty, that, "When a mother touches a body, she touches a person." (2005, p. 92). When two people truly touch and meet, each person's body-mind-soul touches and meet. We intermingle, add, or choke off life with rage, ecstasy, and lust.

Rage and the scream: connection and the furies

Eigen's chapters titled "Screaming" (2002, pp. 151–55) and "Glass house" (2002, pp. 100–105) remain artistic reminders of the linking (and delinking!) reality of our primordial scream; the T-ego and body-ego's primordial amalgam of hunger$\leftrightarrow$ pain$\leftrightarrow$ bliss$\leftrightarrow$ ecstasy$\leftrightarrow$ rage scream as part of our deepest signaling for connection to the Other (and self). Perennial in its essence, rage permeates our history – personally, mythologically, and collectively. We find rage against the imaginary (psychotic anger), rage against the idealized but frustrating other, and rage against the self (-I). The +I (good self) and -I (self-attack, rage against self) friction remain timeless. Think of Freud's tripartite wars. Ego against id, superego against ego, superego against id, ego and superego ganging up against id, and so forth. Hating the Other, hating the self; self-rage, body-rage, distinction–union paradoxes.

MILTON: I feel rage in my eyes, my neck. Rage keeps me separate. A tightening, self-tightening. It creates a felt boundary in my sensations and feelings. Rage keeps me *separate,* fights invasion. Contracting, tensing, tightening, fighting. It *stops* my *mingling* of wires, a *fear of mingling* of wires. I am afraid my poison will be too much. You won't be able to metabolize it … Disintegration protects me from getting absorbed. I'd have given anything for a special bond with my father instead of a black substrate, a black stomach pain that creates a boundary, even though it sucks everything into it. I imagine a special bond would have saved me, make me better. But my imagining is rage.

EIGEN: Rage grows out of a failure of the bond. Rage prevents a better bond from forming. Rage bonds or is part of a bonding process, one of the threads that knit together. Rage rips at the knot it helps create.

(Eigen, 2002, p. 162)

In Eigen's Bionian lens, countless vertices and permutations can be found in + I (+LHK) and -I (-LHK), or + I in relation to -L+H-K. Loving hate, hateful love. I am good, feel good, if I think I love you when you can know and touch my rage. Rage against the self, rage against the Other, rage against God, doing-undoing infinitized in -I.

EIGEN: Where does the rage come from?

BARNEY: It's a reaction to a relation that is broken down. A disconnect. A reaction to disappearance, fear. A disconnect that is overwhelming, intolerable. An intolerable rupture, something broken that can't ever be repaired.

(2002, p. 158)

Eigen frequently returns to Bion's notion of a catastrophic emotional explosion in rage, aspects of personality, and psychic functioning scattered over psychic space after being subjected to a catastrophic impact or an internal eternal "grinder." The result, parts of the psyche as scattered debris (psychic ash); psyche fragments falling far from each other, and the origin of both its creation and destruction. Eigen notationally adds to Bion's lexicon by describing *catastrophic* and *fatal* emotional rage explosions (I scream,[11] a silent forever rage scream, breath-holding fury), catastrophic explosive K (knowing that destroys), holes and vanishing parts in the heart, cancerous rage spots, disappearing-obliterated materials (for thinking) in the psyche's functioning, and other nulling "forever" processes. For Eigen thus,

Rage is trauma
Rage is traumatizing

Rage is fusion
Rage tears fusion
Rage tries to undo separation
Rage is separation
Rage is non-fusion, non-separation
Rage affirms
Rage obliterates
Rage moves from self to self in terror, freezing, fiery fury
(Eigen, 2002, p. iii)

Rage can cauterize our ability to recognize and take in what is missing, the missing that can be experienced as traumatic and traumatizing. Various adaptations coat us to experience rage, and Eigen mentions[12] that rage may also function as a particular hope for intimacy, for the beatific, the ideal, the rip-tear logic of inner vision of the ideal, as well as the impact of the Other's otherness in shredding and puncturing this ideal. The starving self as the foundation to cold-warm rage, slow or demanding rage. Being nourished only to experience painful absence;[13] weaning, lack, disconnection, starvation, injury, a dismissed and a diminished self armored by rage tactics. From compliance to control to *T-ego* and *body-ego rage fits*. Eigen adds, "Rage at being broken, rage at the fixing process, rage at the inability to heal. Rage and grief feed each other" (Eigen, 2002, p. 39). Amae meets sit-down strikes, the terrible twos. Eigen's rage in its many forms is evident in educational rage (the other to learn a lesson), transformational rage (self-other needs to change), battle rage (to control), domination-subservient rage, need rage, dependency rage, and God rage. As part of myth, rage is never-ending and ever-beginning. Throughout history, rage has been part of our dying-and-rising god myths, present in most cultures. Art (visual and written), religion, warfare, and politics all creatively reflect our internal and external struggle to find psychological containers able to work with our never-ending daseinicide tendencies in daily living. Inner and outer containers are needed but frequently falter and fail our rage. Fighting fire with fire, violence with violence, the basis of talionic payback and balance[14] leaves man both driven and in the grip of feverish rage, both celebrated and feared. As daimon, it possesses a god-like power to avenge, get rid of, balance out, settle debts, and annihilate irritants. The original scream starts as our perennial archetypal link: agony-rage and bliss. But in the Z[15] *dimension*, caught within the *Omega function*, rage both signals trauma and will retraumatize. That is, swallowing anger and rage like a Sineater (Daws, 2013b) can see psychosomatic solutions that damage the body-ego-Other in a myriad of ways, and rage at the object may become the rage at the body, body-rage. Seraphs placing a burning coal in Isaiah's mouth to cleanse him of sin may serve as an example:

> *Jean, suffering from burning mouth syndrome*: [Reflecting on her mother's control and intrusion] I got cheeky when I was not allowed to do what I wanted. Mother used to slap me in the face when I did get cheeky... As I sit here, I feel like a coal on fire.

Jean, being devout, taught me the following in our work concerning, psycho-analytically, the primal superego and Fairbairn's internal bad object unable to find, symbolically so, the anchoress Julian of Norwich (c.1342–c.1416) in both her mother and father. A painful lack of divine love, Eigen's dual-union, Elkin's wholesome love, and Eshel's Oneness (2019);

> And the tongue is a fire, a world of iniquity. The tongue is so set among our members that it defiles the whole body, and sets on fire the course of nature; and it is set on fire by hell
>
> James 3:6

> The tongue has the power of life and death.
>
> Proverbs 18:21

Many *burning mouth syndrome sufferers* (and others), similar to Jean as *Sineater,* suffer from *chthonic* rage-destruction injuries as found in Greek myth-ologies, i.e., the violent castration and spilling of Uranus's blood by the Titan Chronos giving birth to the Furies, the Erinyes, the female chthonic deities of vengeance. They were Alecto or Alekto (*endless anger*), Megaera (*jealous rage*), and Tisiphone or Tilphousia (*vengeful destruction*). The Furies represent Eigen's *injury rage*, which is cumulative over one's life. Eigen (1999) describes *injury rage* as follows: "It sediments in the belly of one's being and corrupts muscles, nerves, veins. It not only stiffens one's body, it poisons one's thoughts ... Cumulative rage helps nourish a pessimistic, depressive, semi-malevolent counterpart or undertow to one's official, happier self" (1999, p. 48).

In a most lived way, Eigen's affective triptych describes life as the painful stubbing of one's toe against existence (see 2002, pp. 149–150), finding *T-ego* and *body-ego rage,* outrage at insufficiency; the complex interplay between human helplessness and megalomania. Accepting loss can be difficult, at times insurmountable, and rage may be projected as it boomerangs back into the knowledge of one's insufficiency. How to survive the primordial reality that we remain not only embryonic but stumble along as perpetual toe stubbers? Rage and equipment are in need of commensal links, not symbiotic or parasitic, as they may destroy and implode, leaving behind psychic remnants, fragments of being, even gaps, and nothingness. In Eigen's rich thinking, solace may be possible in *cumulative resonance;* an auxiliary primary process thinker stooped in time.

Cumulative resonance to offset cumulative trauma. It was not anything that could be rushed, this slow baking of emotional faith with a taste of emotional freedom … And after going through something, opening begins again. A growing faith rhythm. This is the core of our work, the very core.

(2005, p. 49)

Notes

1 "This nuclear joy kernel, I believe, is inexhaustible, but so, it seems, are suffering, terror, and rage" (Eigen, 1993, p. 203).
2 See Eigen (2006b, pp. 57–60), for a beautiful description of the hallucinatory aspect of *Lust*.
3 Soft and hard qualities in *Electrified Tightrope* (1993), chapter 10, pp. 105–108.
4 Certainly, as in the case of Schreber, ecstasy is more complex and multilayered. He battled nameless dread, infinite terrors by settling on finding a spiritual path in *feminine ecstasy*. Becoming a woman, the divine bride of God "Something" may start anew, undo his soul murder, his immense terror-rage at God/Father; to be born again in the radiance of God. However, becoming God's bride implies a surrender that competes with terror, rape, and further ways of undoing (in Eigen, 2001, especially p. 38). The case of Eva (see "Training wheels," chapter 8, in *Emotional Storm*, 2005) explores the "erotic charge" with much insight.
5 See Eigen (2001b), pp. 20 and 23 respectively, as Eigen discusses the loss of both his mother and aunt. Tasting our tears, bittersweet, bitter and sweet.
6 Eigen (1986, 1996, 1999, 2001b) frequently warns of the paradoxical effect of psychic growth and its relationship to the death instinct. Please see "Smith's dissolution: peace at last" Eigen (1996, pp. 107–113) describing dreams as psychic warning as well as chapter 8, "Life kills-aliveness kills" in *Faith* (2014b, pp. 77–80).
7 Much emphasis has remained on homosexuality and other perversions when thinking and writing about Sodom and Gomorrah. But by studying the Semitic roots of Gomorah as meaning "deep," "copious water," or even "submerged," and Sodom, from the Arabic "sadama" that means "to fasten," "fortify," or "strengthen" – new psychic meaning may emerge. See Macdonald (2000, p. 52).
8 Again see Eigen's beautiful case of *Sparrow* in *Lust* (2006a, pp. 38–46).
9 See the case of Grace on the use and impact of medication Eigen (2009, pp. 92–93).
10 See Eigen (2016, pp. 44–73).
11 The case of Dan in Eigen (2002, pp. 100–105) serves as a beautiful and instructive case study.
12 See the case of Jeff, in Eigen (2002, pp. 25–39).
13 The *painful absence* and its impact on maturation can be found in Eigen's article "On pre-Oedipal castration anxiety," *International Review of Psychoanalysis*, 1 (1974): 489–498.
14 Eigen's *psychospiritual balance by settling accounts*, see Eigen (2006c).
15 "I suspect part of [the] rage come from the Z dimension" Eigen (2010, p. 28).

Chapter 8

Faith and transformation

Eigen the psychoanalytic mystic

> Hindu, Buddhist, and Christian ideals and methods of detachment, together with their late sibling, scientific objectivity, bear witness to the persistent wish and partial capacity to transcend immediate ties.
>
> (Eigen, 1986, p. 365)

The challenge of being human and Eigen's dream

Faith, spirituality, and the transcendental remain deeply held psychological realities for Eigen.[1] Volumes such as *Flames from the Unconscious* (2009), *Eigen in Seoul* (1–3, 2010, 2011, 2021), *Kabbalah and Psychoanalysis* (2012), *Contact with the Depths* (2013), *Faith* (2014b), *A Felt Sense: More Explorations of Psychoanalysis and Kabbalah* (2014c), *Image, Sense, Infinities, and Everyday Life* (2016), and *The Challenge of Being Human* (2018), all explore in a multitude of ways the importance of spirituality, our human need for the intangible, and the need for wisdom literature so easily dismissed in our modern society as sentimental or non-scientific. Eigen possesses a rare and remarkable ability to not only evoke the inherent mystical of everyday clinical encounters but weave together various religious and spiritual traditions (East and West – Jewish, Christian, Buddhism, Taoism, and more!) with ease, cultivating a unique blend of soul knowledge infused with his central concepts such as distinction–union, rebirth, toxic-nourishment, and much more. Given the importance of the spiritual in psychological formation, and before various Eigenesque themes are explored through various analysands' most private spiritual reveries, I remain touched by the dialogue between Dr. Aner Govrin and Eigen published in 2007 (p. xv) as a sample of Eigen's inner felt sense of the spiritual:

GOVRIN: Do you believe in God?
EIGEN: Everything I have to say about God is written in my books.
  Silence

DOI: 10.4324/9781003002871-10

GOVRIN: Perhaps the notion of God is too intimate and sacred for you that you don't feel you can share it with me

EIGEN: [soft, gentle fatherly touch to shoulder] That's true. It's very sensitive of you to understand that.

(2007, p. xv)

Given such private reverie, how could we as analysts feel, write, if not inquire into our spiritual life's most private, personal, and intimate areas? Given our inherent need for *soul privacy* and accessing Eigen's wisdom and soul-care that illustrates deep and abiding respect for inner spiritual dignity, I will use this chapter in the most personal way. I will select the main psychological areas evident in the previous chapters as central to my reading of Eigen's creativity as linked to spirituality within psychoanalytic sessions as spontaneously given by analysands. The areas include distinction–union, psychic damage, sabbath point of the soul, toxic and wounded nourishment, and the rhythm of faith as analysands find and make use of the *spiritual*. All the analysands mentioned in this section experienced spirituality and religion as needed psychological manna in times of dire mental and physical pain and stressors, given day-to-day adaptational expectations.

The wound that never heals meets the flame that never goes out

I will start with a personal anecdote. I contacted Dr. Eigen after reading *Psychic Deadness* in 1998. While reading Eigen's book for the first time, a most cherished "religious" childhood song reverberated throughout me. I remain somewhat self-conscious about writing that the song was the only song that touched my heart growing up as a Dutch Reformed Christian. Certainly it is more a reflection of my bonding process and soul language, having to escape an inherent strictness given my Germanic heritage and Dutch Reformed perfectionism with known tendencies for punishment and fright. Avivah Gottlieb-Zornberg (2009), Adrian van Kaam (1970), Eugen Drewermann (2006), and Paul Tillich (2014), all combined with Eigen's writing on spiritual reality, supported me to reread and (re-)experience my Dutch Reformedness in a very different way, more commensal to my own soul needs. To return to the heart-song, I quote from the book of Matthew 11:28:

Come unto me, all ye that are weeped and overburdened, and I will give you rest.

Going back to Eigen's first article in 1973 (in Eigen, 1993), "Abstinence and the schizoid ego," the importance of rest when overburdened as for renewal (psychic deadness to rebirth) became a possibility I myself experienced as I read Eigen's book. A suddenly atmospheric inner shift caught me off guard – I was left breathless and wept from a place I forgot. I still do. In the most non-judgmental way, I understood that I am both damaged and alive, alive although damaged, and undoubtedly alive in my damage. Whereas my head and digestive tract certainly do, if not still, belong to the work I have done with three separate gifted psychoanalysts, my respiratory belonged to Eigen's book and Matthew's God song. In time they have grown closer together, tandem better, although they do their work separately too.

A return to the origin: Elkin and Eigen

In numerous book volumes (Eigen, 1986, 1999, 2001a, 2006, 2007, 2009, 2010, 2011,2012, 2013, 2014a–2014c, 2018) and heartfelt book chapters (as an example, see "Alone with God," Eigen, 2005), Eigen's writing remains a living testament to his mentor, Dr. Henry Elkin, even in the spiritual domain. Elkin himself wrote the following on religion:

> Religions aim to restore the psyche, or soul, to the primordial world, *its original habit, to relive there, so as to maintain awareness of various phases of its originary experience.* Of the higher religions, the oriental generally focus upon the initial state of primordial consciousness, prior to its encompassing vital distress and gratification, whereas Judeo-Christianity focuses its culminating phase. The closest approximation to the *total* mystic experience of three to six months of age is doubtless to be found in the realms of religious mysticism and psychosis. However, *all genuine aesthetic, love, and philosophic experiences* are also ultimately rooted in diverse though related aspects of the total mystical experience in infancy; and like the mystical religious experience they may be regarded as personal and therapeutic structuralizations of the primordial vital and mental-spiritual tendencies that become chaotic in psychosis. *The main categories of religion, as well as of philosophic, aesthetic, and erotic sensibility, differ as to which phases of primordial mystical experience emerge to govern the conscious orientation to life.*
>
> (1972, p. 399; emphasis added)

An astounding and inspiring description and observation, theoretically and clinically thickened by Eigen through 30 volumes of writing. The age-old view that man is a "child of God" accurately, though figuratively, applies to the most primordial in being human; "God said, 'you are holy because I am holy.' *The sacred core of human life.* I think I always felt it. I think many people do" (Eigen, 2007, p. 77; emphasis added). Even more profoundly, the categories of religion, our philosophical schools of thought, our aesthetic capacity, and creation, as well as our erotic sensibilities only *"differ as to which phases of primordial mystical experience emerge to govern the conscious orientation to life."* (Elkin, 1972, p. 399). All of Eigen's work, from psychosis, feeling deadened, surviving toxic nourishment even in culture, experiencing ecstasy-lust-rage, and touching on the sublime, all resonates deeply with the *sacred core of human life.* The implications are profound, as described by writers such as Edward F. Edinger, Rainer Maria Rilke, and Carl Jung, to name a few, all of whom influenced Eigen's sensibilities. To accentuate this primordial logic and feel, I include three brief examples of such categories, i.e., a moving sensuous description (as with Eigen's *Lust,* 2006a) from a well-known South African novelist, essayist, and poet, Andre P. Brink (1935–2015), the great Bertrand Russell (1872–1970), and by Dr. Eigen, concerning the spiritual in erotic longing, the spiritual in philosophy-science, as well as the spiritual in going through an experience fully (psychoanalytically), that is, a personal syncretistic Brink-Russell-Eigen sensual-mental-transcendental triptych.

> *Brink on intercourse as the sexual equivalent of prayer:* In both, the need to reach out and connect and the lose-and-find paradox are at their most concentrated. Each much be continually renewed because they are fleeting – and the momentary connection with the Other ... continually creates the need for repetition. Both prayer and intercourse present the human person with a paradox of near unbearable ecstasy and agony. And the confession of sin, and the shedding of clothing are, respectively, the indispensable, obvious condition for the religious and the sexual moment...
>
> (*Standpunte,* 1964)

> *Russell:* Suddenly the ground seemed to give way beneath me, and I found myself in quite another region. Within five minutes I went through some such reflections as the following: the loneliness of the human soul is unendurable; nothing can penetrate it except the highest intensity of the sort of love that religious teachers have preached; whatever does not spring from this motive is harmful, or at best useless ... and that in human relations one should penetrate to the core of loneliness in each person and speak to that. At the end of those five minutes, I had become a completely different person. For a time, a sort of mystic illumination possessed me ... I found myself filled with semi-mystical feelings about beauty, and with an intense interest in children and with a desire almost as profound as that of the Buddha to find some philosophy, which should make human life endurable. A strange excitement possessed me, containing intense pain but also some element of wisdom. The mystic insight, which I then imagined myself to possess has largely faded, and the habit of analysis has reasserted

itself. But in something of what I thought I saw in that moment has remained always with me.

(Russell, 1998, p. 149)

Eigen on Jesus and Job: Jesus's suffering is a distillation of our soul's agony. Jesus goes through absolutely, fully, perfectly, what we go through partially. We tend to abort what Jesus goes through fully. Ingrained limits, constrictions, strangulated areas, we pull back, we short-circuit; we make our suffering less than optimal. Still there are times when we do better, when we dare to suffer our own agony, and at that point something opens, changes, and transposes. The story of Job can be seen in this light. The loss of everything leaves agonized suffering with nothing but the God point remaining. Then a new beginning occurs in our psyche, in new life expressing emotional contraction and expansion, the awesome dramas transcribed in the background of our being involving momentous changes of states, like emotional feeling and emptying into boundless pain and joy. Religion is not just another dimension of our life; it is a different way of living. Absolute guilt blows a massive hole in reality and opens reality, and Jesus allows us to participate in a realm of total experience, inviting us to go through fully what we at best do partially.

(Eigen, 2001 to Norma Tracey, in Bloch & Daws, 2015, pp. 233–234)

In Eigen's various spiritual writings, too rich, nuanced, and voluminous[2] to mention in this single volume, he finds that participation "with," "in," and "within" the realm of total experience is of the essence – a *transcendental* coming together of our inviolable soul kernel, *T-ego*, and *body-ego* in a most profound act of faith.

Faith is a vehicle that radically opens experiencing and plays a role in building tolerance for experience. This is what faith faces, must face … Faith rooted in profound grace, *deeper than catastrophe*, a sense that has an impact on the flavour of our lives. So many sessions are crisis of faith, whether precipitated by hate or love. *Crises in the face of violence done to the soul from within and without: real, but also imaginal in terrifying magnification.*

(Eigen, 2014b, p. 124; emphasis added)

In some analogous sense, we can say that the mad patient is reborn through the therapist. *But here we meet with danger. Where only two are, madness remains. Twoness lends itself to fight-flight-fusion. Two seek a third for arbitration. We ultimately appeal to the one beyond for fairness*

– for justice and mercy. This appeal keeps us honest and able to move past premature closures. One of the psychological virtues of Trinitarian thinking is that it *safeguards the division-unity structure of generativity.* God is not a blank hodgepodge or collapsed morass, but, *whatever else, a relational being in the depths of his own nature, a dynamic movement that supports our openness to revelation and response and requires us to live on the cutting edge of Faith.*

(Eigen, 1986, p. 365; emphasis added)

With faith rooted in profound grace, the cases to follow accentuate the importance of religion and spirituality in recovery from a *shattered identity* (Sam) and *rebirth needs* (Sue), as evident in the various chapters described. Although the cases are from my practice and not directly from Eigen's writing, I hope the reader will "find" Eigen's work as a background of support, as without such support, I would not have been able to act in such *psychoanalytic faith.*

A shattered identity: from religious melancholy to a "putting myself together again"

Sam was referred by his physician with symptoms of severe depression and terrifying fear that he may have schizophrenia. After many traumatic losses *on the way* to adulthood, this creative, sensitive, soulful analysand experienced a shattering of his *T-ego* capacities. Nodal, if not synoptic interactions will be given, illustrating *T-ego* trauma, *T-ego* dissociation, struggles in the distinction-union dialectic, difficulty with *feeling* feelings, and much more:

Sam: I am here due to my shattered identity. Two close friends passing away when I was 19. Then losing my faith at the bible school, losing my place in life … All the damage solidified it, *cemented a painful shattered self-consciousness* (T-ego trauma); it is too much. I am so so self-conscious. What is me, and what would please other people … me and not me. Even treatment with a pastor made me feel worse, as if it was my fault all this happened to me. My thinking became *overdeveloped.* Thinking that felt part of me and not part of me. It is difficult to put into words, but it is as if it became a thing in itself: so many thoughts, perspectives, and ways of being. *My feelings and I got dissociated from my thinking, my mind. How to put it all together?* I began to *overthink* … I could not feel anything, not myself, my *feeling self.* I want to heal my mind and feeling, put my identity back together again. I was *breaking from* myself. *I was broken up and then continuously breaking up.* My introverted identity did not fit in the world. Later I build my identity around being like others, extraverted, anything and all I could hang onto! *The losses, a fatal blow, ripped the core out.* I was living Psalm 88. *My soul unto the grave, the pit.* Had to be "on" and lived in an inner panic, constant internal panic. I grabbed onto things – a sensitive side-wild side split: two parts, and then guilt-despair. Hope deferred makes one heartsick, one's heart sick! I am listening to a writer. He wrote a book entitled *Change in Affection.* Also taking an apologetics course and find it very helpful. *Now I have a gage to work with, a limited compass, with faith and reality.* The mystery of things – like gravity, we can't really see it – only its effects! Faith *and* reality!

Sam and I spend a few moments reflecting on the course's approach and respect for "logic," the "logical," and the very human experience that logic can be wounded, be wounding, and broken. No perfect meta-system exists, although, for some orientation, it may be helpful. Sam longed for spiritual voices and thoughts that could serve as a bridge, i.e., a bridge that could bring together a shattered inner and outer world, head-heart disconnect, his self-God disconnect.

***

SAM: What is seen in the Gospels is how to treat people. John 8. What did Jesus write in the sand? It is left for you to think on, although one sees the effects. People dispersed, and no one got stoned, punished, killed. Justice and Mercy.

LORAY: What is written in the sand for you?

SAM: (Tearful) The Psalms, the emotional, to connect the heart. The book of law and mercy, head and heart! The heartbeat of the Bible ... Bring my feeling and thinking together again ...

****

SAM: I am doing ok, surprised! Cry a lot – it's good to feel. Strange that I have a mind-feeling battle! I wonder why I am not in the psychiatry ward! I went for a walk in the dark, for a swim – I see reality, and it anchors me. Grounds my mind in reality. That movie, *A Beautiful Mind.* It freaked me out; my perception, my reality was off. I became aware of how I would push my mind in directions – pushed too far. If not lining up perfectly – a reality meltdown. I lived off my 19-year-old self way too long! Not the new, I could not perceive the new; my emotions and my thinking were frozen! At 30 – I could not keep living off my 19-year-old self. Not take in anything new. It is shocking that I have a job, a family, children and am not in a hospital or an alcoholic.

LORAY: From 19, the rip-tear of loss and shock, your own beautiful mind could not find a way to live "with" "normal," but *at least you found a way to live "off"* your 19-year-old self and "as" others. Maybe you may *live from* as well.

SAM: That makes perfect sense, perfect sense! Life is so intense for me, it has always been. Extreme, I could not maintain it, and I imploded. How do others do it? Feelings run deep; the agony was too much. I lost my anchors in life, totally, internally, and externally. I could not grow. I did not integrate. From a spiritual perspective, I have been thinking of Isaiah, Hebrews (11:37) where people were sawed in two, and Matthew 27:50–51, a veil torn in the temple when Jesus's spirit left him. Cut in two! I felt like that! I would cry, the pain,[3] on my back, up to my chest, physical and emotional pain, it *struck me* [Eigen's *T-ego and body-ego impacts*] Culture is like that ... so complex. Isaiah's vision to heal and relate to people.

I was thinking here on Elkin's and Eigen's veil between light and dark, unconscious–consciousness, sleep–awake, pristine and primordial awakening, shock, our primordial *T-ego*, and despair. A beautiful description from Eigen served as background:

> We respond so to sunsets because they are magnificent. They touch our core. We respond, too, because of the glow. A glow that signals *The Good*. In psychosis, many signs take on reverse value, signals of catastrophe. I have worked with psychotic individuals from whom colors of the sky, especially sunset and sunrise, break through catastrophic dread and touch *The Good* (e.g., *The Psychotic Core*). A sunset glow can become a sign of *The Glow Itself*, a glow that permeates experience. We have experience with both divine and demonic glow and ache for resolution, hopefully divine. As humans, we must deal with both and make the most of inherent tensions. *For the moment, a sunset (and the many kinds of sunsets of emotional life) can break through the negative.*
>
> (Eigen, 2020, pp. 22–23)

LORAY: Walking in the dark, seeing the sun come up, anchored you in the real. In your body too. For a long time, after the rip-tear, the losses, you felt violently cut in two, like the torn veil in the synagogue. Did you know the Greek for synagogue means synagein, "to bring together" or coming together? The real-unreal exist simultaneously. The mind is like the sun coming up, enlightened, enlightening. Like your beautiful mind, yet you are anchored. It is enormous, evokes awe. Like Isaiah (35:1–10), you are looking forward to, similar to Israel, to return from exile, from feeling split in two. To integrate and connect with yourself, your pre-loss self and life, and people around you, and your deep spiritual self.

SAM: Cry ... That is true ... it is so true ... I was even thinking of World War 2 this week. In a postmodern world, there is nothing good about a Nazi. Postmodern, fatal wound, fatally wounded. A deep longing, a longing to be fulfilled, to exists hurts, to put two together, thinking and feeling, what we think and feel of self and other. I distanced myself from making things practical. Mother Theresa, not the most sensitive person I read. And would not want to be sensitive to work where she did. Is there a balance to love? Interesting. A saint that weeded out sensitivity?

LORAY: Saint to weed out sensitivity?

SAM: You have to! My one friend that died told me what happens in South America to street children – cops shooting children. On hearing it, I slept for ten days! I couldn't go anywhere. It is similar since childhood – hearing the pain in pride – I can listen to it, and it is too much. So much in touch, feelings, buried long ago, buried – I buried my feelings too!

I was hearing, as Sam touched upon his painful torn psyche and reality (his moving into the adult world through trauma), a true Guntripian tragedy ensued, that is, the *sadistic object (Nazis, murderous cops)-self in exile dilemmas (sleep, dead children)* that frequently leads to *T-ego* overdevelopment and affective dissociation as desperate adaptation (Daws, 2013a).

LORAY: I also hear from you, your feeling – it is still there, not dead, just buried! Maybe exiled, given the shocks? Or at a distance, given what your friend told you, it makes sense. You had to, needed to put distance between the catastrophes, the unthinkable, your sensitive feelings and beautiful mind. Going to sleep is helpful as well as burying your feelings [*T-ego and body ego* shutdown, Sullivan's somnolent detachment]. But you woke up again! God took days creating the earth and created rest as necessary – his Son returned in three days; we all need time. Rest and return, especially if things are too much. Even the soul needs a sabbath. [Eigen's breakdown–recovery rhythms]

SAM: Yes! A relief to know this! That it's ok. ... The intensity of it, also to live like that.

LORAY: The pain of feeling split you and the Other in two. Like Isaiah's story. A possibility in you, if you need it – to keep apart, and feel apart from your own feelings especially if your human emotions eclipse your spiritual self, from feelings of purity and innocence. A saint part weeding yourself and others? But we may also not just keep apart, be torn or tear only, but keep "a" part of self and others. See it and hold it as "a" part. [Differentiation in the distinction–union structure]

SAM: Goodness! ... Yes ... bizarre part of it wants to bring it forward more, to talk more about it. Love is deep for me. I find identity there. Since 19, I did not work it out, I imploded. Now I see worldly things, such as finances, etc., as just tools, not wrong; it helps. Goodness, my identity.

my thinking seems 19 years old! I was so lonely, only seeing what others were doing, not me. Could not find me, or my identity in them, in the world! I have a more profound need; it is spiritual for me. Paul's teaching helps me; no dominance, no class, the hierarchy should not exist. That book Change of Affection touched me. Did you know they did conversion therapies! Change identity like that? Change my affection? I spoke to a gay guy about relationships, and it's similar, one guy is gay and one not, same and not.

LORAY: [Further dual-union-differentiation; here I was thinking of Eigen's chapter 1 "Faith and transformation" (Eigen, 2011) and Guntrip's theory on the *masters-slave* and *sadistic object – self in exile units of experience*] Commensal, Paul and Isaiah. Class and difference can cut in two, although being cut in two does not have to be violent, a conversion. Culture can also cut in two, impinge on what you felt. Religion, too, like the pastor's thinking you were exposed to. Being with and being different does not have to include a violent surrender or take over. It can have sameness and difference, mercy and law, as you mentioned, a heartbeat, a thinking heart.

SAM: Yes!!! Cultural changes, movements. God moves like that! *God as becoming.* Although people did not know me really, I must say one thing I liked about myself, I was, like my dad, respectful to women, how he treated my mother (Jesus protecting the woman accused of adultery; Jesus as, according to Elkin, the mediatrix – the balance between mercy and Law), that's a good feel!

LORAY: That is our time Sam …

SAM: Thank you, going to have a root canal looked at. I felt a bump here in my gum. I didn't know it was an infection! They did a root canal a long time ago, so I did not feel anything! I can see in on an x-ray and do have that funny bump! [Laugh, relaxed]

LORAY: Something happening! Your own tongue felt something! We may be exposed to an overwhelming event, a deep infection and by taking out the nerve, our feeling, we cannot know something is wrong. You came to therapy cause you did not seem to feel your feelings. We need to feel to understand and know what "infects us," good and bad. We can see it together with reflection, insight, x-ray, and you bring the things that you sense as feeling-thinking bumps.

*****

SAM: I want to tell you an experience: when I was 14, I had a God experience. I was walking on the beach alone, and it was dark, and suddenly I felt a love from above, I started to sing – it was the most joyous experience – full of love, loved fully. I lost that feeling after all my losses at 19.

LORAY: I sense that the love that felt the most real for you was lost after you crossed the veil into adulthood by losing your close friends, feeling disconnected from the bible school, and living in a world that felt too different, too separate from your mother tongue. The essential and most profound connection, the connection with an experience of God and love, God's love, got sawed in two, so did your mind and you. As you are putting yourself together again, awakening, you are coming back from feeling exiled and buried, similar to Lazarus and Isaiah.

SAM: That is *Truth for me*.

St. John of the Cross, the resurrection principle, and falling up

Sue, a creative and psychologically engaged analysand reflects on the following dream, illustrating the importance of rebirth:

A dream, as before, of being chased. Hiding, fearful, and just as those persecuting me nearly capture me, I started to fly, no, not fly as in a complete ascension, just gaining height, it takes some effort, elevation, no longer in their grasp, but there are also limits to the height, and the space is not wide enough to come through. On the side, there is wiring, and if I bump against the wiring, it sparks and hurts. The sparks are like ions, positive and negative, and they are charged. Something forms around me, cocooned, like a chrysalis, and a tall ladder below me, man on top of the ladder, he is like a first responder, to help me, he breaks an opening in the cocoon, it cracks open, feel he touches my feet and pulls me out this encapsulation, the chrysalis. He knows to do it slowly, given what formed around the body. … Enveloped, the cocoon, similar to the wires, are from the same electrical ions, I am getting shocked coming out. It's a visceral dream, the feel, electrical charges. My *Being* was being charged. After I was out of the cocoon could still not speak, a handling move was evident, cared for, achieved for the greater good; someone tried to feed me, the food – I could not even chew yet. I wake up, an important dream, afraid to not remember it. A cocoon, breaking free. Reminds me of other dreams, getting through portals, a birth canal! I had to look up positive and negative ion s… What it means in nature and when it's man made – usually toxic then! A balance is always needed. Even balanced in the air. It also reminded me of a butterfly. Last stage to being an adult. To escape and be transformed after being cocooned. … Internal transformation, nor run away *per se* anymore … it is not so much external or physical changes, it's internal. … Are the persecutory parts representative of me too? I know they are actually me too! They are also parts not fully *transformed.* ... I know that I usually transform under challenging times, never when things go well. ... New awareness comes with difficulty, through difficulty. Think of St John of the Cross, the *resurrection principle!* Richard Rohr, the book entitled *Falling Up!* Like a dream! Goodness. Rise, fall down, they go together, rise and fall ... like breathing. I have been hit many times in life, pick myself up, when I woke up, that feeling, that electric feeling – was so real, still, feel it! Not uncomfortable, but vibrating newness! So much possibility, like a reverie? No, Reverence! Dreams are like medicine to the soul. Still I am present! Wonder at also about neurobiology here, that electricity made me think of it – ignition, ignited, activated, awakened ... giving birth to the new!

We associate from Sue's drawing, her *wiring diagram*, that it may represent both neurobiological wiring and the tree of life – that we are soul-wired!

SUE: To give birth ... I also want to put pen to paper,[4] not just be on the side anymore.

LORAY: Giving birth to self as the energy flows, using your own mind and creativity.

Eigen[5] *as internal co-visor*: Can you find the place you are born anew each moment? Perhaps one only means revival, a feeling of coming alive, renewal, reanimating, rejuvenating, awakening through sensation, feeling, vision. Images of dying out in agony and coming alive in wonder and joy are part of an expressive sense of resurrection, a rhythm in the psalms and life of Jesus.

(Eigen, in Fuchsman & Cohen, 2021, p. 4)

Notes

1 "If I do not draw from the Holy Spirit on a daily basis, I become a semi-collapsed version of myself" Eigen (1998, p. 163).
2 Eigen's 2011, 2012, 2013, 2014a–2014c volumes all serve as psychoanalytic-spiritual works supporting the development of *spiritual solace equipment*.
3 Echoing Eigen see Horton, Gewirtz, and Kreutter's (1988, pp. 68–70) *The Solace Paradigm*. Eigen's rhythm of faith is written in Horton et al. as developing "solacing equipment," reflected in *spiritual solacing from the Other*.
4 "By comparison, psychoanalysis as a *talking-writing cure* seems eminently sane" Eigen, in Fuchsman et al. (2021, p. 9).
5 Eigen echoing Rabbi Schneerson.

Chapter 9

Epilogue
Eigen's love

> My soul calls to you from the depths, cries the psalms. A part of the heart
> joy, a part of the heart sorrows, dread, rage. Soul beyond hearing, touching,
> indefinable presence touching you.
>
> (Eigen, 2014, p. 124)

Being with Eigen nourishes perennial soul-pain, soul hunger, soul-wondering,
soul-expansion, soul-contraction, soul-connection, soul cries, and more. Eigen
has freely shared with so many his own professional and personal areas of
profound joy, loss, inability, hope, and tragedy. Allowing an inner experience
able to call forth a rebirth of self, developing equipment able to sustain the
vagaries of toxic nourishment and damaged bonds, appreciating a rhythm
of faith in our distinction–union dialectic, welcoming our sensitive self's primordial affects from the depths of the unconscious, and navigating emotional
storms without our over-reliance on control and mastery approaches, have all
been part of Eigen's life-work.

> If we grow enough of a psyche so that we can work decently with our-
> selves, we may be able to become more or less *creative catastrophes*. We
> need to admit the unevenness of personality development.
>
> (1992, p. xvii; emphasis added)

> Little by little, I was transformed by love. I'm far from perfect – I think
> you've seen that. I've shared myself with you. I'm still a mess. I'm a little
> less dangerous. It's not simply learning to modulate your hurtful aspects,
> although that's part of it. It's being transformed inside by a feeling you
> didn't expect to have.
>
> (Eigen, 2010, pp. 52–53)

With Eigen, we continue as *creative catastrophes* in love, far from perfect,
reborn continuously. Eigen, similar to Elkin, Bion, and Winnicott, keeps us
alive in ways furthering F in O. I cannot help but resonate with Eigen's own

DOI: 10.4324/9781003002871-11

written thoughts on Bion and Winnicott as found in the *Electrified Tightrope* (1993), although, with much gratitude, would want to include Dr. Eigen's work as well;

> I have been reading Winnicott for nearly 30 years and Bion half that time and do not find that I am anywhere near exhausting either. What a welcome contrast to many books and articles in the mental health field! Here the human imagination- psychoanalytic imagination- is alive and well. The horrific is endlessly faced. There are no facile exits. Yet psychic life persists, evolves, survives its annihilation, its extinction. Out of nowhere the fire that never goes out flares up, often at the point where no flame seemed to be possible.
>
> (Eigen, 1993, p. xxv)

As we depart, as we must always do, to all the readers, *Namasté*.

> The divine light in me bows to the divine light within you.
> I honor the place in you where the entire universe dwells.
> I bow to the place in you that is love, light, and joy.
> When you and I bow to our true nature, we are one.
> My soul recognizes your soul.
> We are the same, we are one.
> I honor the place in you that is the same as it is in me.

Bibliography

Ayers, M. (2003). *Mother–Infant Attachment and Psychoanalysis: The Eyes of Shame*. Hove and New York: Brunner-Routledge, Taylor & Francis Group.

Bach, S. (1994). *The Language of Love and the Language of Perversion*. Northvale, NJ: Jason Aronson, Inc.

Balint, M. (1968). *The Basic Fault: Therapeutic Aspects of Regression*. London: Tavistock.

Balint, E. (1993). *Before I was I: Psychoanalysis and the Imagination* (Ed. J. Mitchell & M. Parsons). New York: Guilford Press.

Berdyaev, N. (1939/2009). *Spirit and Reality*. San Rafael, CA: Semantron Press.

Berdyaev, N. (1944/2009). *Slavery and Freedom*. San Rafael, CA: Semantron Press.

Bion, W. R. (1957). Differentiation of the psychotic from the non-psychotic personalities. *International Journal of Psychoanalysis*, 38: 266–275.

Bion, W. R. (1959). Attacks on linking. *International Journal of Psychoanalysis*, 40: 308–315.

Bion, W. R. (1965). *Transformations*. London: Heinemann.

Bloch, S., & Daws, L. (Eds.) (2015). *The Living Moments: On the Work of Michael Eigen*. London: Karnac, Routledge.

Bollas, C. (1992). *Being a Character: Psychoanalysis and Self Experience*. New York: Hill & Wang.

Bollas, C. (1999). *The Mystery of Things*. London and New York: Routledge, Taylor, & Francis Group.

Bollas, C. (2011). *The Christopher Bollas Reader*. London: Routledge.

Brandchaft, B., Doctors, S., & Sorter. D. (2010). *Towards an Emancipatory Psychoanalysis: Brandchaft's Intersubjective Vision*. New York: Routledge.

Brink, A. P. (1964). Oor religie en seks (Concerning religion and sex). *Standpunte* 18(2): 33–40.

Casement, P. (2020). *Credo? Religion and Psychoanalysis*. London: Aeons Books Ltd.

Cardinal, M. (1983). *The Words to Say it: An Autobiographical Novel by Marie Cardinal* Cambridge, MA: Van Vactor & Goodheart.

Celani, D. P. (2010). *Fairbairn's Object Relations Theory in the Clinical Setting* New York: Columbia University Press.

Chrzanowski, G. (1973). The rational Id and the irrational Ego. *Journal of the American Academy of Psychoanalysis*, 1(3): 231–241.

Civitarese, G. (2013). *The Violence of Emotions: Bion and Post-Bionian Psychoanalysis* London and New York: Routledge.

Coleman Nelson, M., & Eigen, M. (1984). *Evil, Self, and Culture*. New York: Human Sciences Press.

Corbett, L. (2015). *The Soul in Anguish: Psychotherapeutic Approaches to Suffering*. Asheville, NC: Chiron Publications.

Corrigan, E. D., & Gordon, P.-E. (Eds.) (1995). *The Mind Object, Precocity, and Pathology of Self-Sufficiency*. Northvale, NJ: Jason Aronson, Inc.

Crastnopol, M. (2015). *Micro-trauma: A Psychoanalytic Understanding of Cumulative Psychic Injury*. New York: Routledge.

Daws, L. (2006). Charting the Omega Function: Psychoanalytic thoughts on the quality of the internal object of eating disordered patients. *Issues in Psychoanalytic Psychology*, 28(2): 15–32.

Daws, L. (2013a). Is there anybody out there? The Masterson approach to the schizoid dilemma. *Contemporary Psychotherapy*. http://contemporarypsyhotherapy.org/volume-5-no-1-spring-2013/is-there-anybody-out-there/.

Daws, L. (2013b). The Last of the "Sin Eaters": Psychodynamic reflections on the "Burning Mouth" Syndrome. *International Journal of Psychotherapy*, 17(3): 24–42.

Daws, L. (Ed.) (2016). *On the Origins of the Self: The Collected Papers of Henry Elkin, Ph.D.* Missoula, MO: EPIS Press.

Daws, L. (2021). Healing longing in the midst of damage: Eigen's psychoanalytic vision. In K. Fuchsman & K. S. Cohen (Eds.). *Healing, Rebirth, and the Work of Michael Eigen* (pp. 36–50). London: Routledge.

Drewermann, E. (2006). *A Violent God-Image: An Introduction to the Work of Eugen Drewermann* (Tr. M. Beier). New York and London: Continuum International Publishing Group, Inc.

Dunne, C. (2015). *Carl Jung: Wounded Healer of the Soul: An Illustrated Biography*. New York: Shelley & Donald Rubin Foundation.

Dupond, J. (Ed.) (1985). *The Clinical Diary of Sandor Ferenczi*. Cambridge, MA: Harvard University Press.

Eigen, M. (1973). The call and the lure. *Psychotherapy: Theory, Research, and Practice*, 10(3): 194–197.

Eigen, M. (1974). On pre-Oedipal castration anxiety. *International Review of Psychoanalysis*, 1: 489–498.

Eigen, M. (1986). *The Psychotic Core*. Northvale, NJ: Jason Aronson, Inc.

Eigen, M. (1992). *Coming through the Whirlwind*. Wilmette, IL: Chiron Publications.

Eigen, M. (1993). *The Electrified Tightrope* (Ed. A. Phillips). Northvale, NJ: Jason Aronson, Inc.

Eigen, M. (1995). *Reshaping the Self: Reflections on Renewal in Psychotherapy*. Madison, CT: Psychosocial Press.

Eigen, M. (1996). *Psychic Deadness*. London: Karnac.

Eigen, M. (1998). *The Psychoanalytic Mystic*. London: Free Association Books.

Eigen, M. (1999). *Toxic Nourishment*. London: Karnac.

Eigen, M. (2001a). *Damaged Bonds*. London: Karnac.

Eigen, M. (2001b). *Ecstasy*. Middletown, CT: Wesleyan University Press.

Eigen, M. (2002). *Rage*. Middletown, CT: Wesleyan University Press.

Eigen, M. (2004). *The Sensitive Self*. Middletown, CT: Wesleyan University Press.

Eigen, M. (2005). *Emotional Storm*. Middletown, CT: Wesleyan University Press.

Eigen, M. (2006a). *Lust*. Middletown, CT: Wesleyan University Press.

Eigen, M. (2006b). The annihilated self. *Psychoanalytic Review*, 93: 25–38.

Eigen, M. (2006c). *Age of Psychopathy* (www.psychoanalysis-and-therapy.com/human_nature/eigen/pref.html).

Eigen, M. (2007). *Feeling Matters*. London: Karnac Books.

Eigen, M. (2009). *Flames from the Unconscious*. London: Karnac Books.

Eigen, M. (2010). *Eigen in Seoul: Madness and Murder* (Vol. 1). London: Karnac Books.

Eigen, M. (2011). *Eigen in Seoul: Faith and Transformation* (Vol. 2). London: Karnac Books.

Eigen, M. (2012). *Kabbalah and Psychoanalysis*. London: Karnac Books.

Eigen, M. (2013). *Contact with the Depths*. London: Karnac Books.

Eigen, M. (2014a). *The Birth of Experience*. London, UK: Karnac Books.

Eigen, M. (2014b). *Faith*. London: Karnac Books.

Eigen, M. (2014c). *A Felt Sense: More Explorations of Psychoanalysis and Kabbalah*. London: Karnac Books.

Eigen, M. (2015). O, orgasm and beyond. *Psychoanalytic Dialogues*, 25(5): 646–654.

Eigen, M. (2016). *Image, Sense, Infinities, and Everyday Life*. London: Karnac Books.

Eigen, M. (2018). *The Challenge of Being Human*. Abingdon: Routledge.

Eigen, M. (2020). *Dialogues with Michael Eigen* (Ed. L. Daws). London and New York: Routledge.

Eigen, M. (2021). *Eigen in Seoul*, Vol. 3: *Pain and Beauty, Terror and Wonder*. London: Routledge.

Eigen, M., & Govrin, A. (2007). *Conversations with Michael Eigen*. London: Karnac Books.

Elkin, H. (1958). On the origin of the self. *The Psychoanalytic Review*, 45: 57–76.

Elkin, H. (1966). Love and violence. *Humanitas*, 2: 165–182.

Elkin, H. (1972). On selfhood and the development of ego structures in infancy. *The Psychoanalytic Review*, 59: 389–416.

Eshel, O. (2019). *The Emergence of Analytic Oneness: Into the Heart of Psychoanalysis*. New York: Routledge.

Ehrenzweig, A. (1967/1995). *The Hidden Order of Art*. Berkeley, CA: University of California Press.

Fairbairn, W. R. D. (1952). *Psychoanalytic Studies of the Personality*. London: Tavistock.

Fairbairn, W. R. D. (1984). *Psychoanalytic Studies of the Personality*. London: Routledge & Kegan Paul.

Federn, P. (1952). *Ego Psychology and the Psychosis*. New York: Basic Books.

Ferenczi, S. (1995). *The Clinical Diary of Sándor Ferenczi* (Ed. Judith Dupont. Tr. Michael Balint & Nicola Z. Jackson). Cambridge, MA: Harvard University Press.

Ferrari, A. B. (2004). *From the Eclipse of the Body to the Dawn of Thought*. London Free Association Books.

Ferro, A. (2002). *Seeds of Illness, Seeds of Recovery. The Genesis of Suffering and the Role of Psychoanalysis*. Hove: Brunner-Routledge.

Fordham, M. (1994). *Children as Individuals*. London: Free Association Books.

Fuchsman, K., & Cohen, K. S. (Eds.) (2021). *Healing, Rebirth, and the Work of Michael Eigen*. London and New York: Routledge.

Gibson, K., Lathrop, D., & Stern, M. E. (1986). *Carl Jung and Soul Psychology* New York: Haworth Press.

Giegerich, W. (2020). *What are the Factors that Heal?* New York: Routledge.

Groddeck, G. (1923). *The Book of the it*. London: Lund Humphries & Co. Ltd.

Grotstein, J. S. (1981). *Do I Dare Disturb the Universe? A Memorial to W. R. Bion*. London: Karnac.

Grotstein, J. S. (1987). Making the best of a bad deal: On Harold Borris' "Bion Revisited." *Contemporary Psychoanalysis*, 23: 60–76.

Grotstein, J. S. (1997). Integrating One-Person and Two-Person Psychologies: Autochthony and Alterity in Counterpoint. *Psychoanalytic Quarterly*, 66: 403–430.

Grotstein, J. S. (2000). *Who is the Dreamer that Dreams the Dream? A Study of Psychic Presences*. Hillsdale, NJ: Analytic Press.

Grotstein, J. S. (2007). *A Beam of Intense Darkness: Wilfred Bion's Legacy to Psychoanalysis*. London: Karnac.

Guntrip, H. (1969). *Schizoid Phenomena, Object Relations, and the Self*. New York: International Universities Press.

Hazell, J. (Ed.) (1994). *Personal Relations Therapy: The Collected Papers of H. J. S. Guntrip*. Northvale, NJ: Jason Aronson, Inc.

Hazell, J. (1996). *H. J. S. Guntrip: A Psychoanalytic Biography*. New York: Free Association Press.

Horton, P. C., Gewirtz, H., & Kreutter, K. J. (1988). *The Solace Paradigm: An Eclectic Search for Psychological Immunity*. Madison, CT: International Universities Press.

Kalsched, D. (1996). *The Inner World of Trauma: Archetypal Defenses of the Personal Spirit*. London: Routledge.

Kalsched, D. (2013). *Trauma and the Soul: A Psycho-Spiritual Approach to Human Development and its Interruption*. London: Routledge.

Kafka, F. (2007). In the penal colony (Tr. Stanley Corngold.). In *Kafka's Selected Stories* (pp. 35–59). New York: Norton Critical Edition.

Kafka, F. (2017). *Letter to my Father*. London: Alma Classics.

Keleman, S. (1989). *Patterns of Distress: Emotional Insults and Human Form*. Berkeley, CA: Center Press.

Khan, M. R. (1963). The concept of cumulative trauma. *Psychoanalytic Study of the Child*, 18: 286–306.

Khan, M. R. (1972). Dread of surrender to resourceless dependence in the analytic situation. *International Journal of Psychoanalysis*, 53: 225–230.

Kohut, H. (1971). *The Analysis of the Self*. New York: International Universities Press.

Kohut, H. (1977). *The Restoration of the Self*. New York: International Universities Press.

Langs, R. J. (1976). *The Bipersonal Field*. Northvale, NJ: Jason Aronson, Inc.

Langs, R. J. (1977). *The Therapeutic Interaction: A Synthesis*. Northvale, NJ: Jason Aronson, Inc.

Levinas, E. (1969). *Totality and Infinity*. Pittsburgh, PA: Duquesne University Press.

Little, M. I. (1990). *Psychotic Anxieties and Containment: A Personal Record of an Analysis with Winnicott*. Northvale, NJ: Jason Aronson, Inc.

Lombardi, R. (2017). *Body–Mind Dissociation in Psychoanalysis: Development After Bion*. London: Routledge.

Macdonald, B. (2000). *East of the Jordan: Territories and Sites of the Hebrew Scriptures*, vol. 6. Boston, MA: American Schools of Oriental Research.

Masterson, J. F. (1972). *Treatment of the Borderline Adolescent: A Developmental Approach*. New York: Wiley-Interscience.

McDougall, J. (1980). *Plea for a Measure of Abnormality*. New York: International Universities Press, Inc.

McDougall, J. (1989). *Theatres of the Body: A Psychoanalytic Approach to Psychosomatic Illness*. New York: W. W. Norton & Co.

McDougall, J. (1991). *Theatres of the Mind. Illusion and Truth on the Psychoanalytic Stage*. New York: Brunner/Mazel.

Milner, M. (1969/2010). *The Hands of the Living God: An Account of a Psycho-Analytic Treatment*. London: Routledge.

Murdin, L. (2021). *Psychoanalytic Insights into Fundamentalism and Conviction: The Certainty Principle*. New York: Routledge.

Neumann, E. (1954/1989). *The Origins and History of Consciousness*. London: Maresfield Library.

Ogden, T. H. (2009). *Rediscovering Psychoanalysis: Thinking and Dreaming, Learning and Forgetting*. London: Routledge.

Robbins, A. (1986). *Expressive Therapy: A Creative Arts Approach to Depth-Oriented Treatment*. New York: Human Sciences Press.

Rothenberg, R. E. (2001). *The Jewel in the Wound: How the Body Expresses the Needs of the Psyche and Offers a Path to Transformation*. Asheville, NC: Chiron Publications.

Russell, B. (1967 [1998]). *The Autobiography of Bertrand Russell, Vol. 1: 1872–1914*. London: George Allen.

Sechehaye, M. (1951a). *Symbolic Realization*. New York: International Universities Press.

Sechehaye, M. (1951b). *Autobiography of a Schizophrenic Girl*. New York: Grune & Stratton.

Shengold, L. (1999). *Soul Murder: Thoughts about Therapy, Hate, Love and Memory*. New Haven, CT: Yale University Press.

Spielrein, S. (2019). *The Essential Writings of Sabina Spielrein. Pioneer of Psychoanalysis* (Ed. R. I. Cape & R. Burt). London: Routledge.

Spitz, R. (1965). *The First Year of Life*. New York: International Universities Press.

Stein, M. (1993). *Mad Parts of Sane People*. Asheville, NC: Chiron Clinical Series.

Tausk, V. (1933). On the origin of the influencing machine in schizophrenia. *Psychoanalytic Quarterly*, 2: 519–556.

Tillich, P. (2014). *The Courage to Be*. New Haven, CT: Yale University Press.

Ulman, R. B., & Brothers, D. (1988). *The Shattered Self: A Psychoanalytic Study of Trauma*. Hillsdale, NJ: The Analytic Press.

Van Kaam, A. (1970). *On Being Involved. The Rhythm of Involvement and Detachment in Human Life*. Denville, NJ: Dimension Books.

Volkan, V. (1976). *Primitive Internalized Object Relations*. New York: International Universities Press, Inc.

Volkan, V. (1995). *The Infantile Psychotic Self and its Fates: Understanding and Treating Schizophrenics and Other Difficult Patients*. Northvale, NJ: Jason Aronson, Inc.

Watts, A. (1989). *The Book: On the Taboo Against Knowing Who you are*. New York: Random House, Inc.

Watts, A. (2009). *The Book: On the Taboo Against Knowing Who you are*. London: Souvenir Press.

Wheeley, S. (1992). Looks that kill the capacity for thought. *Journal of Analytical Psychology*, 37: 187–210.

Williams, G. (1999). On different introjective processes and the hypothesis of an "Omega Function." *Psychoanalytic Inquiry*, 19(2): 243–253.

Williams, P. (2010). *The Fifth Element*. London: Karnac Books.

Williams, P. (2013). *Scum*. London: Karnac Books.

Winborn, M. (Ed.) (2014). *Shared Realities: Participation Mystique and Beyond*. Skiatook, OK: Fisher King Press.

Winnicott, D. (1955). The metapsychological and clinical aspects of regression within the psychoanalytic set-up. *International Journal of Psychoanalysis*, 36: 16–26.

Winnicott, D. (1965). *The Maturational Processes and the Facilitating Environment*. London: Hogarth.

Winnicott, D. (1967). The location of cultural experience. *International Journal of Psychoanalysis*, 48: 368–372.

Winnicott, D. W. (1969). The use of an object. *International Journal of Psychoanalysis*, 50: 711–716.

Winnicott, D. (1971). *Playing and Reality*. London: Routledge.

Winnicott, D. W. (1974). Fear of breakdown. *International Review of Psycho-Analysis*, 1: 103–107.

Winnicott, D. (1975). *Through Pediatrics to Psycho-analysis*. London: Hogarth.

Winnicott, D. W. (1984/1990). *Deprivation and Delinquency* (Ed. C. Winnicott, R. Shepperd, & M. Davis). London and New York: Routledge.

Winnicott, D. W. (1988). *Human Nature*. London: Free Association Books.

Wurmser, L. (1981). *The Mask of Shame*. London: Johns Hopkins University Press.

Zornberg, A. G. (2009). *The Murmuring Deep: Reflections on the Biblical Unconscious*. New York: Schocken Books.

Index